Teen Moms
The Pain and the Promise

I must confess that the title of this book initially turned me off. I thought I was in for yet another excuse-filled, blame-society melodrama that asks readers to empathize with irresponsible girls who go out and get themselves pregnant. Well, Evelyn Lerman disabused me of my skepticism and introduced me to the real world of teen pregnancy.

In their own voices, the teen moms in Lerman's excellent book assess themselves honestly, neither sparing themselves nor their mates, many of them adults. And Lerman's wise and unemotional observations offer a viable blueprint for society to take real responsibility in educating everyone, especially males, involved in this enduring problem. Without doubt, this book is a forthright, sensitive addition to a body of literature that too often paints teen moms as either victims or whores. Lerman explores the problem in all of its complexity.

Bill Maxwell
Editorial writer and columnist
St. Petersburg (FL) Times

Teen Moms
The Pain
and the Promise

By Evelyn Lerman

Illustrated by Jami Moffett

Morning
Glory
Press

Buena Park, California

Library of Congress Cataloging-in-Publication Data

Lerman, Evelyn, 1925-
    Teen moms : the pain and the promise / by Evelyn Lerman.
        p.   cm.
    Includes bibliographical references and index.
    ISBN 1-885356-24-2 (hc) . -- ISBN 1-885356-25-0 (pbk.)
    1. Teenage mothers--United States. 2. Teenage pregnancy--United
States. I. Title.
HQ759.4.L47 1997
306.874'3--dc21   97-20134
                                                                CIP

MORNING GLORY PRESS, INC.
6595 San Haroldo Way   Buena Park, CA 90620-3748
(714) 828-1998   FAX (714) 828-2049
Printed and bound in the United States of America

Contents

Preface   7

Foreword   11

Introduction   18

1   Start with Statistics — The Realities   30

2   Why Have Sex So Early?   36

Trends in early pregnancy • Lack of male role model • Molestation, rape, incest are *not* rare • Older men — teen women • Mothers who can't cope • Parenting siblings • Who needs a man to raise a child? • Peer pressure also a factor • Are the pregnancies intentional? • Other factors • Summary.

3   Teen Moms' Feelings About Men   60

Effects of sexual abuse • "He said he loved me" • Violence is increasing • Older men as predators • Neglect and desertion • Risk of AIDS • Positive attitudes for some • Summary.

4　　**The Meaning of Motherhood**　　　　　**80**

Following through on promises • Will the poverty
continue? • Education seen as a way out • Does past
abuse affect mothering? • The Needle

5　　**The Worries Come Swiftly**　　　　　　**98**

Being a good mother • They worry about health
• "Will my child be safe?" • Problem of money
• And other worries . . . • Why didn't they think *first?*
• Advising younger teens • Do they understand what
parenting means? • Teen moms' list of don'ts

6　　**Feelings about Welfare and Independence**　**114**

"End welfare as we know it" • "I'd rather work"
• Considering society's role • What happens now?

7　　**Changed Lives —**
　　　　The Pain and the Promise　　　　　**130**

"How has your life changed?" • Some see positive
change • Can teen pregnancy be an improvement?
• What works?

8　　**We *Can* Affect Their Future**　　　　　**144**

Creating a team for teens • Lobby for education
• Innovation in education • Group homes needed
• Updating the laws • Changing workplace
policies • Importance of personal involvement
• Mentoring values • Changing roles of mothers
• Modeling relationship skills • How do we
mentor? • You *can* change lives

Afterword　　　　　　　　　　　　　　　**167**

Appendix　　　　　　　　　　　　　　　**169**

Description of Interview Group　　　　　　**171**
Becoming a Lobbyist　　　　　　　　　　**172**
Research Citations　　　　　　　　　　　**175**
Bibliography　　　　　　　　　　　　　　**183**
Index　　　　　　　　　　　　　　　　　**189**

Preface

Why did a retired school teacher, camp director, school personnel director decide to write a book advocating open-mindedness about teenage mothers? You might think it fit with my child-oriented careers, and you'd be right. But that's only part of the story. The other dimension, an even more powerful motivation, is the force of the love and admiration I have for my own mother and the quality of her mothering.

A dressmaker, the breadwinner for and essentially the single mother of three daughters, she raised us with her talented hands, her loving heart, and her bountiful soul. She loved us so hard that we still feel her warmth now, thirty years after her death. She worked so hard that I still find my greatest joy in work. She poured so much of her soul and spirit into us that no day is complete for me unless I have reached out to someone in a personal way. Perhaps my interest in teaching came from my dynamic first teacher, my mother who escaped a Jewish ghetto in

Russia in 1918 and fought her way to America, her 18-month-old first child in her arms and her sick husband by her side.

"Anything is possible," she told me. "All it takes is hard work and faith, faith in yourself and faith in a greater force than yourself." For her that faith was her God. She talked to Him and He helped her.

For me that faith is in the force of humanity, the "more-than-me-ness" of good people who care about others.

I believe that when you're born lucky, you can do anything. That kind of luck means being born to a mother who loves you with all her heart. She loves you when you're bad and when you're good, when you fail and when you succeed, when you love her back and when you don't. That's lucky.

But everyone is not lucky. Some mothers can't give that kind of love. They may be too beaten down by poverty and not have the resilience to fight. They may have been so abused or neglected themselves that they don't have a positive role model to guide them. They may be so stuck in their own needs that they can't reach out to a new life. They may be addicted to drugs or alcohol or they may be victimized in other ways.

What, then, happens to their children? Some, the lucky ones who find other loving adults to care about them, make it to adulthood relatively unscathed, but the others fall into the same patterns as their mothers did. They learn what they see. They get into early sex, drugs, victimization, and hopelessness. And so the cycle continues.

When I first began this writing, it was about my mother and the qualities of good mothering which she demonstrated. My mentor, Bob McGrath, a teacher, encouraged me to share those ideas with teen parents.

My thoughts went out to these young women, a few of them as young as 12 or 13, many of them 14 to 16 years old. What was happening with them and their babies? I decided to find out.

In the course of two years I interviewed 50 pregnant and parenting young women, ranging in age from 13 to 23. As they told me their stories, common threads emerged.

They'd been raised by mostly single mothers, some previously married and divorced or deserted. Many, though not all, of these teenagers had been sexually abused; some, though not all, had been physically abused. But practically all had been emotionally abused, either through neglect, too early and crushing responsibility for younger siblings, or by over-zealous parenting which had not allowed for any freedom of movement or expression.

Though they had not been lucky before they got pregnant, many considered themselves lucky now, even though they knew they were too young to be mothers. They felt they'd been rescued by their pregnancy; they'd been rescued from their own ghettos of poverty and neglect. They were now getting an education in alternative schools which met their needs and where they had found loving, caring adults, essentially new mothers, in their teachers and counselors.

Their pre-pregnancy friends no longer mattered to them. They were out of gangs, they'd given up on drugs, shoplifting, and sleeping around. They had a purpose in life larger than themselves, and they had people to light their way.

In reading this book I hope you will come to believe, as I do, that these young women are not society's trash. They are not bad girls or criminals. They are young people thrashing about in search of better lives, not so much for themselves as for their children. "Accept us," they are crying out. "We can do it if you will love us."

As a society we can answer this call for help. Yes, money is part of the answer, but even more important is the gift of ourselves. We can help to provide the nurture they lacked, we can "be there" for them so they can "be there" for their children. If we make it work for them, we'll make it work for us. "You get what you give," my mother used to say. "One hand washes another."

Please read these stories and take another look at teenage mothers. Can we, together, break the cycle?

Evelyn Lerman
July, 1997

Foreword

Evelyn Lerman entered my life when I was having great difficulty responding without anger to those people who blame teenage mothers for the woes besetting our society. Some people were saying too much of our tax money goes to support "those girls" who, of course, "have babies in order to get their welfare checks." "They" also said teen moms are promiscuous and they wondered why teen mothers don't "just say 'No'."

Yet one of the first things my students taught me when I started teaching school-age parents was that relying on welfare for financial support was *not* the way they wanted to live. In fact, I quickly learned that one of the best uses of my tax money was to help teenage parents continue their education and workforce preparation. Staying in school, which sometimes required financial assistance, was their ticket to getting *off* the welfare rolls. Many were also in a monogamous relationship when they became pregnant, and that relationship sometimes endured in spite of their ages. As for saying 'No,' research studies in various states show the majority of teen moms were sexually molested as children. As one teen mom expressed it, "How do you say 'No' when you never had a chance to say 'Yes'?"

As I continued to hear these comments, I was becoming more and more incensed at the blame society was heaping on these young women. I was also not pleased, to put it mildly, with the harsh realities of the welfare reform movement. I became angry toward the people who didn't understand the world so many teen parents face, a world of poverty and abuse.

All this information swirls around and mixes with my feelings of caring, love, and hope for the teenage parents I have known. Getting angry about an issue doesn't, by itself, help anyone. Feeling strongly about issues, however, can lead to positive action toward needed change. And that is what *Teen Moms: The Pain and the Promise* does. The book effectively illustrates the harsh realities so many teenage mothers face. Evelyn Lerman's purpose in doing so is to provoke her readers to strong feelings about our responsibilities, as individuals and as a society, to make our world better for young people, those who already have children and those who, with help, may delay pregnancy and parenting until they are ready.

Teen pregnancy prevention — from the President to our neighbors, prevention is the important goal. We agree. *Preventing* too-early pregnancy works better for everyone — teens, their families, our entire society. Spending our energy, our resources, and our creativity on prevention makes sense.

But should these prevention efforts focus only on teens? One would assume so from reading the goals and objectives of many teen pregnancy prevention groups around the country. But why are these goals so often directed *only to teens?* An obvious answer: We're talking about *teen* pregnancy. Of course we focus on teens. The catch? Pregnancy involves two people. More than 500,000 teen women give birth each year. The majority of their sexual partners, however, are not teenagers. The majority are adult men.

The conventional wisdom that teen pregnancy is a *teen* problem bothers me a lot. Since the majority of the fathers of the babies born to teenage mothers are adult men, it seems more rational to call teen pregnancy an adult problem in which teens are also involved. I haven't seen much in the media recently urging adult men to "Just say 'No'."

To be effective, teen pregnancy prevention efforts need to focus on *both* partners. In fact, in other areas of life, we expect adults to take *more* responsibility than children. Shouldn't the adults involved in teen pregnancy be considered responsible for those pregnancies? Judging from those goals pointing at changing only teens' behavior, you'd think "those girls" got pregnant by themselves.

Prevention curriculum and activities *for teens* need to focus on helping teenage men understand their responsibilities toward younger women. Focus also needs to be, for both parents, on parenting so that their male children grow up to respect girls and women, and to understand that sexual intercourse carries with it an awesome responsibility toward one's partner, especially if that partner is younger.

Teenagers who are already parents, fathers as well as mothers, need our help. Enhanced educational services are critical for school-age mothers and fathers. For some, social services and financial support are a necessary bridge toward building independent and productive lives for themselves and their children.

Evelyn Lerman talked with, interviewed, and interacted with teen moms for more than two years. She also did a thorough research review on the subject. *Teen Moms: The Pain and the Promise* is a wonderful mix of the research together with the realities of individual teen mothers. She finds that for some adolescent mothers, the pregnancy has turned their lives around — for the better. The tragedy is that the realities of their growing-up years make the poverty, overwhelming responsibilities, and worries of very early parenthood appear to be an improvement.

Teen Moms: The Pain and the Promise is not meant to imply that all teenage mothers were sexually abused as children, or that all were poor, or all the fathers of their babies are adult men. Teen pregnancy can happen in any of our families. When I was teaching in a teen parent school program, my students came from upper-middle class families as well as from families surviving on welfare grants. Some had been sexually molested, but certainly not all. Some had apparently healthy relationships with young men who were their peers. These facts, however, do not conflict with the picture of poverty and abuse portrayed in this book. Each teen parent is a unique individual. *Teen Moms* focuses on the realities faced by the majority of teenage mothers in the United States today.

Most important, *Teen Moms: The Pain and the Promise* does not stop with the "Ain't it awful?" picture. Many of the teenage mothers quoted here have had a childhood that we would never choose for any child. Our task is to work toward better lives for these young parents *and* for the children, all of our children, so that early pregnancy will not be the route to a better life than they have had. That better life needs to start at birth and continue throughout adolescence.

Evelyn's suggestions for each of us as individuals and as we work together can make a difference. She is absolutely right in stating that it will take all of us working together to turn the pain of too-early pregnancy into the promise of a better life. Even more important, we can help young people avoid the pain of early pregnancy by going directly to that promise of a better life.

Jeanne Warren Lindsay, Author
*Books, Babies and School-Age Parents: How to Teach Pregnant
     and Parenting Teens to Succeed* (co-author, Sharon Enright)
Teen Dads: Rights, Responsibilities and Joys
Teens Parenting four-book series

Acknowledgments

I know now why we have to push our children to write their thank-you notes. It's hard to say thank you on paper. It's easy to show gratitude with a hug or a kiss or a handclasp, but when we have to put our feelings on paper, it's two-dimensional. The words may not sound real. So, depending on our relationship, consider these thank-yous a hug or a kiss or a handclasp, and know that I know that without your cooperation and interest, *Teen Moms* would never have been born. Thank you to

. . . the young women who took me into their lives and shared their stories. I have used pseudonyms to protect their privacy, so I cannot list them here, but they are the soul of this book.

. . . my mentor, Bob McGrath, a teacher, who spotted a book in my writing . . . my editor/publisher, Jeanne Warren Lindsay, who recognized a book in the making . . . my friend, Sarah Sellinger, who read, critiqued, and guided my heart, my head, and my hand.

. . . the administrators who opened their schools to me: Sharon Abrams, Maine Children's Home for Little Wanderers,

Waterville, Maine; Nanette Dizney, Teenagers as Parents
Program (TAPP), Bradenton, FL; Catherine Christiansen, Our
Mother's House, Venice, FL; Pat Hartstein, Harris Teenage
Information Program for Students (TIPS), St. Petersburg, FL;
Sister Gloria, Solve, Bradenton, FL; Barbara White and Lorraine
Colby, Cyesis, Sarasota, FL; Lynn Breskus, Alpha House, Bra-
denton, FL . . . the teachers and counselors who assisted me and
shared their expertise: Joanne Bailey, Jodi Perry, Gael Anderson,
Kathleen Witton, Bea Moran, Michael Epstein, Jim Oliver, Andy
Tartler, Colleen Taylor, Carole Leslie, Barbara Stegeman.

. . . Dr. Sandy Gordon, whose insights as a writer moved me
in the right direction; Lois Goodman and Joan Rubinstein who
used their time and talents to work with the teens I interviewed.

. . . Max Schilling, whose interest, faith, knowledge of the
data, and materials kept me going.

. . . Congressman Dan Miller of Sarasota, Florida; Suzanne
McQuarry of Kennebec Valley Community Action Program,
Waterville, Maine; Cheryl L. Klein, Birthline, Catholic Charities
of Maine; and Margaret Ricker of the Maine Children's Alliance
for the materials they so generously shared.

. . . Nettie Bailey, whose success story of her rise from daughter of a sharecropper to entrepreneur inspired me to further
research . . . Gail Sheedy, Dr. Karel Cooperman, Helen Faye
Rosenblum, Lil Grossman, Dr. Lee Pickler, my granddaughter
Rebecca Gang, Evelyn Clark, Barbara Young, Arlene and Ron-
nie Klein, Vivian Greene, Ruth Brinn, Toots and Bill Rau, Ted
and Babs Gilbert, Dr. Philip Warren, Dr. Alan and Muriel Small,
Charlotte Laven, Barbara and Dick Levy, Dr. Jack Bornstein,
and Dr. Harold Blinder who shared either their viewpoints on
teen pregnancy or on my writing about it.

. . . my writing colleagues in Maine and Florida, who talked
with me, discussed ideas, read drafts, and were honest in their
appraisals of the work in progress . . . and thank you to all whose
ideas, thoughts, and suggestions buried themselves into my
consciousness, but no doubt emerged as I was writing. Please
forgive me if I have not mentioned your name.

Evelyn Lerman, Sarasota, Florida

To
Albert Lerman, my dear husband,
who ran interference, ate leftovers,
produced the data bases,
and held me together.

Introduction

"**E**verybody trashes teenage mothers!" they said. I leaned forward in my chair, making eye contact with each speaker, straining to hear every word. "They call us whores. They say we have no morals."

"They say we're irresponsible. That we have babies just for the welfare and food stamps. That we're school dropouts. That we're lazy and no good."

"They say, 'Where are your morals?'"

"They ask, 'Why aren't you married?' They're prejudiced against us just because we're young and single and because we have babies."

"They don't know anything about how we lived before we got pregnant, or how we live now."

"They say we're bad, but they don't know how hard we're working to be good mothers."

We were sitting in a circle of chairs in a classroom in an

alternative high school in a mid-sized city in a southern state, these teenage girls and I. Their babies were in the nursery in the next building. I was astonished that this was their overwhelming concern. I had been interviewing teen mothers for almost two years, and I had heard their stories. I had heard about abuse and neglect, about poverty and pain, about loneliness and fear.

I had heard that they loved their babies and wouldn't give them up for the world, but that they wished they had it to do over because they were too young to be mothers. I had heard how weary they were trying to finish high school, to prepare for a career, and to be good mothers. I knew how they were struggling with their pasts, their presents, and their futures, and how they mourned the loss of their own childhoods. But they had never before expressed their pain about the way society was stereotyping them.

They were all different. They were African American, white, Hispanic, Native American, racially mixed; they were as young as 12 and as old as 18. Some were breathtakingly beautiful, some were gangly teenagers, and some were children with grown-up faces. They ranged from petite to powerful, from painfully thin to uncomfortably obese, from dull-eyed and inert to bright and articulate.

Different as they were, they all had the same concerns. They were so young in many ways, but so old in others. No matter what their socio-economic background, their race, their physical characteristics, their mental abilities, or their emotional states, they were a sisterhood in their shared early motherhood. And always, the things they said to me were the same.

I had been meeting with pregnant and parenting teens over the course of two years in six different settings for teenage mothers, three alternative high schools and three group homes. I interviewed them in a northeastern state and in a southeastern state, in rural settings and in urban settings. They talked about their childhood and their own mothers. They told me what they worried about and what they wished for, and they seemed brave and tired.

I sensed a sadness in them which I thought was because they knew they were too young to be mothers and were mourning their own lost childhood. I knew they had plenty to worry about, trying to finish high school and be good mothers at the same time, and I knew they had had some terrible experiences in their own lives as children. I heard some anger in their stories, and I heard resignation and determination, but I never put it all together until this day when their hurt feelings bubbled over. They could cope with anything poverty and teen parenting held in store for them, but not with the rejection and disapproval of the adult world.

The next week I met with another group, this time in a small rural town in the same state, to check my perceptions of what I had heard. They talked to me with the same intensity. "They trash us. They call us whores."

"They say, 'Where are your morals? Why did you have sex so young? With your whole life ahead of you, why didn't you have an abortion or put your baby up for adoption?'

"'What are you doing about money? How will you manage?'

"'You're a school dropout. What kind of example will you set for your child?'

"'All you want is welfare and food stamps.'

"'You're too young. You're irresponsible. You're no good.'"

I asked them, "Is any of this true? How would you answer these accusations?" They said:

"Sure we were young, but things happen. You go with the crowd. Our mothers had us young."

"Mine was 15."

"Mine was 14."

"Mine was 16."

"Mine was 18. But they dropped out of school and we aren't.
We're here, going to school, getting an education, working to get
off welfare because we hate it. It makes you feel bad, and
anyhow it isn't enough. We run out in two weeks and the check
comes monthly."

"We need to work, but you have to be 16. And if we are old
enough, it's hard to find a job with benefits. Without health
insurance, we'd be in real trouble with our babies. And you can
only get Medicaid health insurance if you're on welfare. So
we're kind of stuck all around."

"If we can find a good job we take it, and then we go to
school, work, and try to be good mothers, too. It's hard, but we
got ourselves into this and we'll just have to get ourselves out.
That's why we don't do abortions and we don't do adoption. We
got pregnant and we'll make it work."

"In this school we're learning about drugs and alcohol and sex
education. We're not doing drugs and we're not running with the
crowd any more. Most of us don't even date. I think my hormones changed after I had a baby. I don't even care about guys
right now and I don't think I will for awhile. I need all my
energy for my baby and for me."

"Unconventional mothering can be good mothering. Being a
good mother doesn't depend on marriage or having a partner. It
has to do with love, with personal striving."

"It also has to do with the way you were parented. If it was
good parenting and you did well, you learn from that. If it was
bad parenting, you have to learn from that, too. But whatever
you do with your book, be sure to tell them that we're not trash."

One young woman put it exceptionally well. She talked about
how she works so she won't have to depend on welfare. She also
goes to school. "Still there are some people who look down on

me because I'm young with a baby and not married," she said. "I feel bad about that because I'm a good mom and do everything for my daughter.

"One night my baby was having trouble breathing, so I brought her to the emergency room for her asthma. I knew it was the right thing to do, but they were nasty. I knew it was because I was young. I was really upset about that.

"There are some people who respect me for being a good mom, going to school, and doing everything I can for my child, and I appreciate that, but the others really hurt me. I don't do drugs or drink, and I go to school and work hard. I don't see my old friends either, because they're into things I don't want to do. My boyfriend gave up drugs when I told him it was them or me."

Was I onto something? I felt sure I was, but I thought I'd check with professionals in the field who had been working with these girls a lot longer than I had. Each corroborated the girls' feelings. It wasn't paranoia — it was real. They told horror stories of men calling out on the street after these young women as they were leaving school. They called them whores and yelled, "Got any of that for me?" The adults who work with teen mothers told me a large part of their work was trying to build self-esteem into these young people, enough for themselves and their children. Without self-esteem, these professionals feel there is no way to break the cycle of poverty and dependence.

Another group, in another alternative high school in the South, told me, "We're not whores and we're not dropouts. We're still going to school and getting an education so we can support our kids. Welfare doesn't do you much good anyhow, and it's not enough to get by. You run out in two weeks."

"The worst is we feel ashamed to take welfare. We want to work, but you can't get a job if you're not 16, and if you are old enough it's really hard to go to school, be a good mother, and work, too. But lots of us are doing it."

"The thing that's really bad is that if we're not on welfare, we can't have Medicaid for our babies. If we could get a job with benefits, that would work fine, but most of the jobs we can get don't give benefits."

"How can they say we're too young and we're irresponsible?" they continued. "Most of us raised younger brothers and sisters because our mothers were working and we had no fathers at home. By the time we were teenagers we'd already raised a kid or two."

"And about being an example, my mom had me at 15, and she told me not to do it, but I did anyhow. I hope my daughter won't get pregnant so young, and I'll talk to her about it, but who knows. The biggest influence is the other kids anyhow. If they're having sex she'll probably do it, too."

"I wouldn't put my child up for adoption and I certainly wouldn't get an abortion. If I got pregnant, then it's up to me to have the baby and take care of him or her. If God didn't want me to have it, I wouldn't have gotten pregnant. Age isn't what makes you a good mother, it's maturity. And we're maturing fast. You have to when you're a mother. There isn't time to be a kid anymore."

Adults I interviewed who worked with these teens agreed with the girls' perceptions, as did stories in the news. Sharon Abrams, the director of the Maine Children's Home in Waterville, put a real success story in the newspaper. The reactions she got from the public upset her. She told me, "When we publicize cases where the kids have made it, we're told we're glorifying teenage sex. We're also told, if we didn't have this program, kids wouldn't have babies. Nonsense."

Nanette Dizney, the director of TAPP (Teenagers as Parents Program) in Bradenton, Florida, said, "We were in a building that was an old car inspection station, with two rooms for the babies and one large classroom. The county had telecommunications on the other side of the building. The men there were installers of radios for police cars and such. They insulted the girls. They intimated they were whores, yelled at them.

"Juvenile Detention was across the street. The boys could see through the fences and they yelled lewd and nasty things at the girls. 'Give me some, baby.' Most girls were angry although a few liked the attention.

"Even here at this school, we get blamed for anything that goes wrong just because of who we are. Society has a stereotypical bias — if you're 16 and you have a child, you're a whore. The girls, white and black, even call each other 'ho. They internalize the stereotyping. We work on self-esteem. We have two young college students here today, two role models, a black football player who is in pre-med and a white track star studying to be a computer programmer. They're telling the girls their stories, hoping they'll see they can do it, too."

Kathleen Witton, a counselor at an alternative high school, Bradenton, Florida, told me, "People see teen parents through blinders. Stereotyping and bias guide their thinking. Their own experience gives them a point of view that doesn't allow them to see and understand what it must be like to grow up the way these kids do. They can't get beyond it. They're missing an empathy gene. These kids have been through, and some continue to go through, neglect, poverty, physical and sexual abuse, lack of understanding by their mom, and a legal system that just doesn't get it either."

"Write your book about this," the teens said. "Tell them out there about us. Tell them we're not whores, and it makes us feel bad when they say we are. The talk shows are the worst. Tell our stories so they won't hate us so much. Let them find out what we're really like. Just because we're teens doesn't mean we can't take care of our children. We can and we do. Good mothering doesn't depend on age; it depends on attitude."

At that moment, all of my research came together. I had planned this book for teen parents, a forum in which they could share their stories with each other and hear from successful adult women who had been teen parents, but they said, "No, don't write it *for* us, write it *about* us for *them*. They have to know so they won't be so prejudiced against us and our children. We want our kids to have a chance in the world. We don't want them to feel bad about what people think of them the way we do."

That's what this book is about. It's an opportunity for you — the voters, the taxpayers, the policy-makers, the general public — to gain insight into young mothers. You will read their words as they talk about why they had sex as young teens, how they felt when they found they were pregnant, how they feel about being young mothers, what they feel about being on welfare, what their hopes and aspirations are for their children and themselves.

They express their feelings about the men in their lives — their own fathers, the men/boys who were their sexual partners (or who abused them), the baby's father — how pregnancy and motherhood changed their lives, why they didn't choose abortion or adoption, and how they are struggling to be good mothers.

They give advice to younger teens, though they don't think they will listen.

Included, in addition to the teen stories, are insights from professionals who work with these young women, the results of questionnaires I gave to groups, data which has been gathered by various organizations, and commentary from books and articles by educators, social service providers, researchers, and the general public. In the last chapter, I present some ideas about what society can do about this issue. Is it a problem or a new cultural norm? And either way, what is the role of the individual and what is the role of society as a whole?

Start
with Statistics

When I was a little girl my mother used to caution me not to do certain things by saying, "Don't do that. They'll say I'm not a good mother."

"Don't eat too much at someone's house. They'll say I never feed you."

"Don't forget to wash your ears. They'll say I don't keep you clean."

When I asked her who "they" were, she'd say, "People," and I never figured out who these people were. But *they* obviously mattered to her, so *they* began to matter to me.

As I heard the teens telling me their feelings when "they" criticized them, I realized that public opinion still mattered. In spite of the changes in lifestyles and mores in the 90s, these young women were as uneasy with the critique of society as I had been sixty years earlier. What a surprise this was to me! Now I know who "they" are. They're the people who gather in groups and discuss teen pregnancy; they're the writers in the newspapers; they're the participants in the talk shows on the radio and TV; they're the people sharing the world with these teen parents, and they're really worried. They're all of us, and they matter. They are concerned, and they are saying so.

What are "they" saying?

- More teens are having sex and they're too young for sex.
- They don't think it's wrong to have sex before marriage.
- They don't even want to get married.
- More and more babies are being born to teen mothers every year.
- They get pregnant because they want someone to love them.
- They make terrible mothers.
- They want babies just for the welfare checks.
- All the unwed parents are teenagers.
- Their parents aren't supervising and controlling them.

These statements reflect concern for the babies of these young parents; they reflect annoyance with what they perceive as loose morals; they reflect disgust with an assumed lack of responsibility; they reflect anger that their tax dollars are being used for people whom they see as feeling entitled to this help; they reflect fear at what is happening to the values they hold dear.

Are they right? To find out whether perceptions matched realities, I consulted the research. This chapter highlights both.

They say: More teens are having sex and they're too young for sex.

The reality: No, more teens are *not* having sex.

A study released May 1, 1997, by Secretary of Health and Human Services Donna E. Shalala, announced that the percentage of teenagers who had sexual intercourse had declined for the first time after increasing steadily for more than two decades. The 1995 National Survey of Family Growth found that 50 percent of women 15-19 had ever had intercourse, compared with 55 percent in 1990, 53 percent in 1988, 47 percent in 1982, 36 percent in 1975, and 29 percent in 1970.[1] Of interest, too, is the fact that very few of the youngest teens have voluntary sex, and more than half of all teens remain virgins until they are 17. Some do not have intercourse at all during their teen years.[2] Professionals who work with teens agree that adolescents generally are not ready emotionally for a sexual relationship.

They say: They don't think it's wrong to have sex before marriage.
The reality: That's right. They don't.
One-third of the teens surveyed said they thought it was a mistake because of the danger of AIDS and the possibility of pregnancy while two-thirds said it was all right to have sex before marriage. None expressed a moral aversion. In fact, 96 percent of teenage women who have sexual intercourse for the first time are unmarried.[3] An interesting corollary is the adult survey mentioned in *Sex and America's Teenagers* in which only one-third of the adults said sex outside of marriage was wrong. Others, however, worried about sexually transmitted diseases and pregnancy among sexually active young people.

They say: They don't even get married.
The reality: It's true.
Fewer teens are getting married in the 90s than married in the 60s. First births to unwed mothers aged 15-17 have risen from 33 percent of total births in this age group in the 1960s to 81 percent in the 1990s,[4] an exact reflection of the trend in adult women.[5]

**They say: More and more babies are being born to teen-
age mothers every year.**

The reality: The figures keep changing. From the highs of
the 1960s the numbers declined in the 70s and 80s. In the early
90s the numbers began to rise again, but there has been a down-
ward trend in the last few years.

When we look at the 15-19-year-old age group, we see a
decline from 62 births per thousand in 1972 to 50 per thousand
in 1986, then a trend back up to 60 per thousand in 1990.[6]
Among the 15-17-year-olds the rate climbed 23 percent from
1985 to 1994 — from 31 per thousand to 38 per thousand. But if
we look at only the last four years, the birthrate in the 15-19-
year-old group has dropped three percent.[7]

What is true for all age groups and over all of these years is

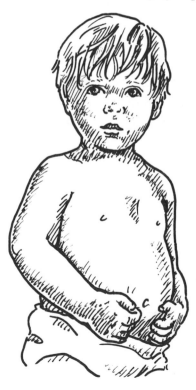

that more and more babies are
being born to *unwed* mothers,
both teen and adult.

**They say: They get preg-
nant because they want
someone to love them.**

**The reality: Only in some
cases, perhaps 15 percent of
the total.**

One million teens get
pregnant every year, and
slightly more than half give
birth. In this group, about 85
percent of the pregnancies are
unintentional.[8] For many, either
the sex has been coercive[9] or the
inexperienced teen has not had
access to or information about
contraception.[10] Most of the

fathers are not teens, but older men — the younger the female, the older the male.[11]

They say: Poor babies! Teens make terrible mothers.
The reality: It takes an exceptional younger teen to be a good mother, and she needs a lot of help.

Most teen mothers are born and raised in poverty, and the cycle continues with their children. These babies tend to have lower birthweight, more childhood illnesses, more infant mortality, poorer medical care, suffer more from hunger and malnourishment; they are exposed to more violence, and have more delayed development than children born to older mothers.[12]

In addition, the mothers are more likely to be high school dropouts, though this has declined,[13] and their lifetime incomes tend to be much lower.[14] All these factors, combined with their youth and inexperience, contribute to difficulty with parenting.

They say: They want babies just for the welfare checks.
The reality: Only a few have babies to collect welfare.

Consider these facts: Seventy-four percent of the women who experienced initial sexual intercourse before age 14 and 60 percent of those who had sex before age 15 report that the sex was involuntary[15]; Mike A. Males, author of *The Scapegoat Generation,* reported that childhood sexual abuse was the single biggest predictor of teenage pregnancy over the past forty years[16]; the National Campaign to Prevent Teen Pregnancy reports in its Prospectus that 85 percent of teen pregnancies are unintentional. It's hard to equate these facts with the idea teens have babies to collect welfare.[17]

Yes, welfare serves one-seventh of all United States children, and some of the mothers chose to have a baby knowing that welfare would help them out.[18] However, 14 percent of the babies born to teens are born to the "working poor," families in which one or both parents work but are still below the poverty

line. Another piece of information: Medicaid pays for prenatal
care and childbirth, but does not pay for abortion.[19]

They say: All the unwed mothers are teens.
The reality: This is not true.

Though 70 percent of teenage mothers are unmarried, they are
still a minority in the general population of single mothers. Adult
women account for the majority of single mothers.[20] In fact, the
proportion of unmarried births to adult women has increased
fourfold in the last twenty years.[21]

They say: Teens' parents aren't supervising them or controlling them.
The reality: A large proportion of teens' parents either don't or can't even when they try.

A large proportion of the United States' 24 million teens live
in poverty, a condition which results in difficulty with providing
the basics of food, clothing, and shelter. Nearly forty percent of
the 15-19-year-olds in this country are poor or low income,[22] and
many grow up in economic, social, and ethnic ghettos. A working mother with young children needs to spend 21 percent of her
income on child care; most can't afford it.[23]

Living in a two-parent household is associated with a decrease in the likelihood of teen pregnancy, but the percentage of
single-parent families has risen. In 1970, out of all families with
children, 10 percent were headed by a single parent; by 1992, the
figure was much higher.[24]

One-third of 15-year-olds report that their parents never
talked to them about sex and pregnancy, and one-half said a
parent had not discussed birth control or sexually transmitted
diseases with them. When parental influence is low, peer influence is high. In the absence of a strong relationship with a
parent, if friends are having sex, a teen most likely will do the
same. Twenty-five percent of 13-17-year-olds felt pressured by

their peers to experiment with sex.[25]

The issues people are worrying about are very real, even if all of the perceptions are not. But why is all of this happening? Why are teens having sex earlier? Why are more engaging in premarital sex? What do they think about men? Why are so many women — adult and teen — choosing not to marry? What about welfare? What kind of mothers are these teens? What's happened to parental supervision and control? What is the promise for the future?

In the chapters which follow, these issues and questions will be explored in depth.

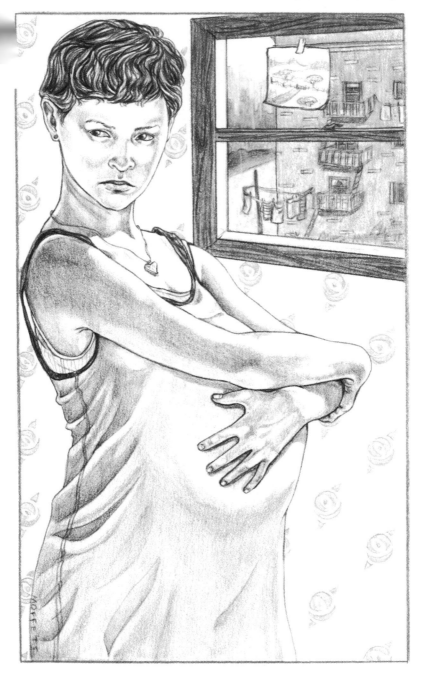

Why Have Sex So Early?

Everyone asks the questions. "Why are children having children? What are they doing having sex so early?" You hear it at gatherings, on talk shows, in professional meetings — wherever people are talking about conditions in America today. What is the reason children, some as young as 12, are having sex, and sometimes getting pregnant as a result? The answers are complex. Many theories are expressed by adults who work with teens, by researchers in the field, and by the teens themselves as they tell their stories.

The social workers, psychologists, and educators answer by talking about teen feelings. They cite neglect, abuse, and society's mores as causes. They say loneliness and lack of self-esteem are the result. They talk about peer pressure, absent fathers, single mothers, sexual and physical abuse, alcohol, drugs, male predators and crushing burdens of responsibility on teens. They mention adult role models from movies, TV, and sports having promiscuous sex and bearing children without being married.

"Nobody's been there to set limits for these girls," says Gael Anderson, a nurse and health education teacher at an alternative high school. "But after they get pregnant, and especially after they have their baby, they begin to see the consequences of their actions. Too bad they couldn't see it before their lives got changed so radically."[1]

Trends in Early Pregnancy

The researchers give us an even broader perspective. They talk about trends, trace the history of the United States from 1940 to 1993, and point out the economic realities of the 90s. According to Mike A. Males, author of *The Scapegoat Generation,* these were years of upheaval in sexual mores. He cites a depressed wartime birthrate, the postwar baby boom, the sexual revolution based in part on the widespread use of the birth control pill and the legalization of abortion, the increase in divorce and unwed births, and the steady decrease in the age of puberty.[2] He also notes that the increase in the unmarried birthrate among women aged 20-44 was reflected in the increase in the unmarried birthrate among teen women (ages 15-19). The adult behavior was imitated by the teens.[3]

Poverty with its attendant issues is at the core of the teen child-bearing problem. Six out of seven of America's teenage mothers were poor before they gave birth. In fact, the teen birthrate in a given decade can be calculated in advance by looking at the child poverty rate of ten years earlier.[4] This, with 90 percent accuracy!

Judith S. Musick, who authored *Young, Poor and Pregnant,* attests that poverty is even more influential than race or ethnicity.[5] Adolescents get pregnant from all groups, of course, but it is the teens from lower socio-economic groups, the children of poverty who do not have other options open to them, who most often deliver and raise their children.[6]

The fifty teens I interviewed, unable to discern cause from effect, unaware of the societal and economic forces that were shaping their lives, talked about people. They told me about the men, women, and peers in their lives. Jacqueline, Tanya, Ruby, and Tracy talked about their absent fathers:

Jacqueline, 16: *I think I'm okay emotionally somehow because I've been through a lot in my life, even before this, and I learned how to take it. My parents are divorced, and I live with my mom. My father got a new family and has his wife's two children now.*

When he got married again he told my brother and me he'd see us when he sees us. I was seven then. He still brings child support to my mother, and he talks to me when he comes, but I don't think he really cares about me.

Tanya, 18: *Mom had her first child when she was 18 and divorced my father when I was three months old. I never saw him when I was real little, but I remember him coming to visit when I was two. I was in my room crying, and he came in and picked me up. But I never saw him again until this year when I was eighteen.*

In the eighth grade I was curious about what it would be like to sleep with a guy. I was

14 and he was 15 and we thought it would be fun.

I thought I was in love. I knew I could get pregnant, but I didn't care and I didn't use protection.

I have three kids now. I live with my mom and I'm finishing high school. We're doing fine.

Ruby, 16: *I have a good baby and I'm a good mom. We don't have a dad with us, not my dad and not the baby's dad. My dad is in the Army. I saw him last when I was four, and I really miss him. I don't know if I'll ever see him again. Momma has people looking for him and trying to locate him for me and the baby, but no luck so far.*

That's why I'm glad we're moving to the state my baby's dad lives in so my son can grow up with his dad. We plan to marry when we get older, but we're too young now.

Tracy, 16: *My parents were divorced when I was 8. I don't talk to my dad. My brothers do, but I don't like him and I don't see him. Great-grandpa is 92, and this baby will be the fifth generation in this state.*

Great-grandpa is amazing. He makes things from rocks. He's neat. He's very strong still, but I don't know if he's strong enough to hear that I'm pregnant. I haven't told him. He's very set in the old ways and very religious. He dresses every night for dinner with Great-grandma. I'm not going to tell her either because her mind isn't all there.

My life was good. So how come I got pregnant at 15? It just happened. The luck of the draw. I was lucky it wasn't earlier because I was 14 when I started having sex. Here in this state the guys are real fast. It's put out or get out. Lots of parties. We didn't do drugs, though.

Each of these teens expressed a sense of loss because she didn't have a father. He was either gone when she was little, or divorced from her mother a few years later. Even Jacqueline,

whose father comes to visit and brings child support, doesn't feel
she really has a father. It appears that whether the absent father
shows interest or is totally absent, the perceived loss is real and
deep.[7] These young women feel rejected, even if the dad is
making an attempt to see them.

Lacking communication with a close, loving, positive male
role model, teens approach their sexuality with insecurity and
doubt. According to Musick, "The feelings, thoughts, and actions
of these adolescent girls can be understood as logical outcomes
of their attempts to cope with father absence."[8]

My own adolescence surfaced when I read these words. We
were three girls raised by a working mother, living with an
invalid father. He was frequently absent, either in a hospital or
living in a warm climate which he hoped would be better for his
rheumatoid arthritis. When he was home we couldn't afford to
pay for his care, so we took care of him ourselves.

I can still smell the herbal infusions I used to cook up to make
hot packs for his swollen legs and stiff neck. I'd run from the
kitchen stove to his bedroom to apply the hot towels, the steam-
ing cloths burning my fingers. But if I let them cool, they
wouldn't be hot enough to help him. I could see he was grateful
for the relief the heat brought his aching body, but I remember
feeling that he thought it was my job and I really shouldn't
expect thanks.

Basically a good man, he was so consumed by his illness that
he was emotionally separated from us. I felt like a stranger, a
caregiver, not a daughter.

I grew up in this matriarchal household believing that men
were weak and women were strong. And I also believed, given
my limited experience, that strong women made men weak. This
was my fear when I dated and when I married. Would the real
me — with the strengths, the weaknesses, the drive, and the fears

of men and what I might do to them — destroy my relationship? Fortunately, the man I married was strong enough to be his own person and to allow me to be mine. The distance from adolescence to adulthood offered me a clearer understanding of male/female relationships, so we've made it together.

This recollection, surely nothing to compare with what today's impoverished teens are experiencing, made me think more deeply about teens who grow up either without strong, loving male role models or with male models who are alcoholic, drug addicted, abusive, violent, or neglectful. How do they define themselves in relation to males?

Lack of Male Role Model

The professionals and researchers agree that the lack of positive male role models is a significant factor in early sex and pregnancy. Nanette Dizney, director of an alternative high school, cites this lack as typical among teenage parents,[9] as does Max Schilling, Teenage Parent Program Specialist, Florida Department of Education, Tallahassee, Florida.[10] Males cites "the upsurge in divorce" between 1940 and 1993 as one of the contributing factors in the rise of unwed teenage births.[11]

We know there are fathers who, in spite of divorce, support their families with both emotional and financial assistance, and that the daughters of these families can grow up whole and secure. But the overwhelming number of divorced fathers of adolescents, especially among the teen mother population, do not provide child care or child support, and the children suffer the consequences.[12]

We might begin to think, then, that nothing could be worse for young girls than not having a father in the home. It turns out that the absent father may not be as damaging to his daughter's feelings of self-worth as is the presence of a sexually abusive father, stepfather, uncle, older brother, or mother's lover who lives in the home. The absence of a caring and responsible father figure goes beyond the psychological realm into the issue of the safety and security of the children in the home.

Children without an adult male to protect them run a greater risk of sexual molestation. Two-thirds of the teen mothers in a 1992 study had been sexually abused or raped by a parent or other adult male. The offenders' mean age was 27.4 years.[13]

Try to imagine the lingering effects on teens who have been sexually abused, who have experienced rape, or who have been forced into incestuous sex by a family member. If society has any questions about the importance of daughters having a supportive and sustaining relationship with their fathers, these stories should answer them.

Jenine, 16: *I never knew my real dad. Mom told me a little about him, but she was never married to him, and by the time I was born he was gone. I sat across a room from him once, but I decided I didn't want anything to do with him by then.*

Mom is married for the third time now, and I'm glad to have a good man in the house because my first stepfather abused me. He started when I was about 5 and never quit until he left the house when I was 11. I never said anything to my mom because I was so embarrassed and frightened by him.

At 14, when I got to be a teenager, and I had the normal problems of a kid that age, all the stuff that had gone on in those years came back, and I freaked out. I ran away from home. I stayed just anywhere or I stayed with friends. Anytime anyone touched me it triggered memories and I got freakier. I thought I could run from it but of course I couldn't.

Rosalyn, 23: *I want to forget the vision of my brother, plunging, hurting. Emotions scarring me, ruining my spirit. It's like larvae that gets inside you and eats you up from the inside out.*

*I want to ignore the world, pretend that castles and Prince
Charmings do exist, that love lasts, that feelings are true.*
*   I was sexually abused by the babysitter's son when I was 7.
My brother raped me when I was 8. It colored my thinking
about men, and I've never felt secure about my relationships
with guys since then.*

Molestation, Rape, Incest Are *Not* Rare

As fervently as we would wish that rape and incest were rare,
the National Women's Study of 4000 women in 1992 learned
that one-eighth had been raped, a projected 12.1 million, two-
thirds of them before reaching 18, and one-third of these before
they were 11.[14] Most survive, but their legacy is early parenthood, memory loss, poor self image, loss of childhood, a too-
early adulthood, and painful memories of abuse.

Why would a young woman who had been sexually assaulted
as a young girl want to have sex at 13 or 14, or even older, I
wondered. The question haunted me. Wouldn't she be disgusted,
turned off, frightened?

Two counselors at alternative high schools, one with twenty
years of experience, told me that although you'd think that a girl
who'd been sexually abused wouldn't want any part of sex, it
seems to work the other way. They don't feel they're good for
much, but if somebody wanted them enough to force it on them,
they must be good enough for that. Their low self-esteem gets a
boost if somebody pays attention to them, expresses love or
caring, and wants to have sex. So they do, and many of them get
pregnant.[16]

Dr. Debra Boyer of the Women's Studies Program at the
University of Washington in Seattle agrees that the effects of
sexual abuse in adolescence are linked to early sex. She writes
that sexual abuse affects children in all areas of development.
They are at higher risk for mental health and social functioning

problems than are non-molested children.

Victims see themselves as living in a world of unpredictable or uncontrollable events, a world in which actions have no rational consequences. Such young women are at higher risk for adolescent pregnancy. Dr. Boyer's research found that 62 percent of the pregnant and parenting teens she interviewed had been sexually molested or raped prior to their first pregnancy.[17]

Older Men — Teen Women

Male predators are another risk factor for young female teens.[18] Because of their youth, inexperience, need for attention, and poor self image, they may be vulnerable to adult male predators at rates that mock the notion that most teenage sex resulting in childbirth takes place between teenagers. Fifty percent of the fathers of babies born to teenage women are five or six years older than the mother. Two-thirds of these males are 20 years of age or older.[19] Even more revealing is the statistic that the younger the teen, the older the male.[20]

Fran, 18: *I lived alone with my mom. I met the baby's father at a concert last year, and I couldn't stand him. But when we began to go places and have fun, I liked him better. He was 24 when I was 17, and he had money. He was in college. One night he stayed at my house and we had sex. I got pregnant.*

Fran fits the profile of the teen who is trapped and thinks the older male is a way out of her situation. Now she lives at home, another generation of single mother with her child. But this is not sexual molestation, you will say. No, it sounds more like a willingness on Fran's part.

The problem is that what a teenager sees as a way out (older male, some money, perhaps some education) turns into a one-night stand, which the father may forget and the mother lives with for the rest of her life.

Mothers Who Can't Cope

As tempting as it may be when we hear the teens' stories, we can't place all the blame for early teen sex on men, bad, good, or indifferent. Mothers of teens have a role, too. The teens talked about their mothers' alcoholism, physical abuse, drug abuse, prostitution, and — far less dramatic, but equally debilitating — just plain neglect.

Ginger, 13: *Mom's an alcoholic, so life with her was hard. During the week when she was working, things weren't too bad. But then the weekend would come, and she'd really let go with the drinking. Things were very bad then. She'd get verbally abusive and lose control of herself.*

I knew when I told her I was pregnant she'd hit the roof, and she did. She was fifteen when she first got pregnant and decided to have the baby adopted. When she got pregnant again she was 22 and thought she'd better get married. That ended in divorce when I was two. I really never saw my dad much then, except summers, and I haven't seen him recently, not since I was nine years old.

Mom married a second time, but got divorced from that husband when I was eight. So fathers haven't been a big part of my life.

Gail, 17: *My sister and I lived with my mom, and we lived in lots of places. Finally we settled here, hoping things would be better. But Mom was still doing drugs and prostitution, and it didn't look like things would improve. I was into drugs, too, and I had missed a lot of school with that and all the moves.*

One night, about a year after the move, we had a big argument. I wanted to go to school but she wanted me to stay home and help her after an operation she had. We fought about it and she went out, probably looking for guys and booze. My sister and I were hungry so we went out shopping for food.

We got home and were fixing something to eat when she came in drunk and started throwing the food around the kitchen. We couldn't help laughing at her because she looked so funny, and she got so mad that she threw us out. She crumpled our clothes into piles and threw them and us out on the street. The neighbors called the cops, and CPS (Children's Protective Services) *sent us to foster homes.*

Irma, 16: *When I was growing up my mom was wild. She had all different kinds of boyfriends and dragged us around to wherever she was going. My own father was not ready to settle down, she told me, and she wasn't ready to stay home and take care of us either. She's the kind who worries about herself and her current boyfriend, but doesn't worry about my sister or me.*

Parenting Siblings

Another situation that has been both cited by researchers and recounted by teens has to do with too-early parenting of siblings. When single mothers who are not poor need to leave home, whether to work, to date, or to do errands, they hire a babysitter. When mothers living in poverty, even the working poor, need to leave home, they put their oldest child in charge of the younger ones. These babysitters, still children themselves, tell their stories:

Adrienne, 17: *I have been grown up so long that I don't even want to be a kid anymore. I lived with two different grand-mothers and my mom, all at different times in my life. We really never had a dad, so I never knew enough to miss one.*

When I lived with my mom, I wasn't really happy because I was only a kid myself, and I became the babysitter. I was scared about the job. And I wanted to go out and play, but

I had to babysit. I wanted freedom, but my mom didn't understand that at all. She was studying to become a nurse, and she made it. Even though I know she had to do what she did, I resented it then, and I think I still do.

When the smaller kids finally got old enough to be left alone, I didn't even want to go out anymore. I had no friends to play with, and by then I had stopped asking her to let me go out, so I've never been to a football game or to a basketball game, and I only recently started to go out to movies. I went to one school dance, but I was scared and alone, and it wasn't any fun. So I'm not afraid of losing my freedom when my baby is born because I never had any anyhow.

Anne, 21: *I wanted to go out and play with the other kids, but no, I had to stay home and babysit my brother again. I wouldn't have minded if I thought my parents really cared about me, too, but I knew they didn't because when they finally got home from work they never talked to me about anything except my brother. How was he? Did I take good care of him? I could have thrown something at all of them.*

*Then my father would go pour himself one beer after
another "to relax," and my mother would get busy in the
kitchen or the laundry, and that would be the end of my time
with them.*

*When I was 12, I finally found someone who paid attention
to me and expressed his love for me. We became lovers, and
at 14 I had Robbie. I guess taking care of my brother helped
me in some ways because I knew a lot about taking care of
Robbie when he was born. I know how lonesome and unloved
I felt, and I make sure this doesn't happen to my son.*

Tammy, 14: *When I was four my mom didn't take good care of
us. She was on drugs, cocaine and crack, and she'd go out
and never come home. I had two sisters younger than me, and
I was taking care of them as best I could. I diapered them and
tried to feed them. My grandpa, he was an alcoholic, but he
taught me how to change diapers so I could do it. My oldest
brother was out with friends all the time, so I was the only
supervision they had.*

*I knew my mom needed me, and I knew Grandma treated
her awful. She fought with her. So did Mom's sister. She tried
to run Mom over with a car, and I felt I had to help her.
Grandma cursed my mom even when she was trying, but they
get along better now.*

Being a mom myself at 14 isn't hard.

Shunika, 18: *And where was Mom? Like Dad, she worked days
and many nights to try to keep the family going in our small,
poor, rural town. They really tried, I see now, but the problem
for me was that I had a younger brother, and he needed to be
cared for. So when I turned eight and he was five, I became
his mom. I'm proud to say I did a good job for him — he's a
good student, a good athlete, and best of all, he has self-
esteem. He thinks he's great, and he is.*

For me, though, I was too young to be taking care of a little boy. I needed a mom myself, and she just couldn't do it. Even when she was home, she couldn't get up the energy, or maybe she didn't know how, to talk with me and listen to me. So I lived with my modest successes, and what I saw as my terrible mistakes, feeling guilty and blaming myself for not doing better.

Neither parent ever had — or made — the time for us, and I never heard anything good about myself. I was never told by either one of my parents that I was pretty, or smart, or would amount to much. So I fell for the first boy who came along and told me I was pretty and smart, and that's how I got pregnant at 17.

My parents were sure I would never amount to anything. You tend to believe your parents, and I guess I thought they had it right.

Adrienne, Anne, Tammy and Shunika were all fearful. They were deprived of their freedom when they were just learning how to use it. They wanted their own lives, but they were tied down to a responsibility they weren't ready for. They couldn't make friends of their own, the business of childhood, because they had to take on the business of adulthood, becoming acting mothers when they were still children. In adolescence, since mothering was how they were valued most, why not have their own babies? They were developed enough to conceive them.

It's too late to be a kid anymore, they realize, and they don't even know how to be. Might as well do what they know how to do. They were important in that role once; they could be again.

The interesting thing about these young women is that they are a lot more resilient than their peers who didn't have these responsibilities, but who had been neglected by their mothers and fathers or sexually abused by their fathers or other men.

These nurturing teens had developed some sense of personal worth in their caretaking role.

Hope Edelman, author of *Motherless Daughters,* confirms this. She says that their previous experience helped them prepare for some of teen motherhood's demands.[21] My question is how well will they be able to sustain parenthood, these young women who have been so deprived of their own childhood?

Who Needs a Man to Raise a Child?

The research also tells us that teens whose mothers were single when they gave birth are more apt to become single mothers than other teens.[22] The single mother is the only female role model the teen knows. Her mother was young. Why shouldn't she be? Her mother did it alone. Why can't she? Who needs a man to raise a child?

Candy, 18: *I like being a mom. I always wanted to be a young mom. Mom was 16 when she had me. She understands me because she's young, and I want to be like that with my daughter.*

I was 16 when I started having sex. He was 21. But that broke up fast, and I didn't have sex again until I met the father of my baby. He's 18, too, and he's a good guy. Our baby is 6 months old. I knew I could get pregnant, but I didn't worry about it because I really wanted to have a baby.

Mindy, 16: *"Don't get pregnant at 16 like I did, Mindy." That's what my mom used to say to me from the time I was 13. She'd say it over and over, but she didn't say much else. In fact, she didn't talk to me at all. I was aching to talk to her about that and about other stuff that kids worry about, but she never had the time. Just time for "Don't get pregnant at 16 like I did, Mindy."*

Why should I listen to her, I thought. She doesn't really

care about me. So you know the story. I got pregnant at 15.
When I was a kid I remember feeling pretty good about myself
most of the time, but then something bad would happen and
all the good feelings would be gone. That's how it is now.

Peer Pressure Also a Factor

And what role does peer pressure play? How many times have
we, as parents, heard our children tell us that "everybody's doing
it"? It turns out that peer pressure is more important for some
teens than others. Being lonely and feeling neglected by the
parent or parents who are at home leads many girls to try to find
friendship and love "out there."

Jim Oliver, a social studies teacher at an alternative high
school, having worked with adolescents for 30 years, tells us that
the peer groups know how to pick out likely recruits. They spot
the young teens who are needy. They have a knack for knowing
who's looking for affiliation. They know which kids will resist
the pressure and which kids won't. They reach out to the teens
who need affirmation that they are attractive and worthwhile,
and who, if they can't get it at home, will search for it in
their peers.

The teens become part of a group, and follow the standards
set by the crowd. If the crowd is drinking or doing drugs, they do
it, too. If the group is having sex, they will, too. Oliver says that
a strong, loving relationship with a parent is the best defense
against peer pressure.[23]

Jewel, 17: *My mom still thinks it was her, but it wasn't. It was*
me. I was a spoiled kid, and I wanted my own way. When I
couldn't get it, I did whatever I needed to get it. So when
things were awful at school, when the girls pushed me
around, and when I started fighting with my mom over
everything, I just left home.

I was 14, kind of young, but I knew I had to get away from

*the fighting and I had to have control over my own life. I had
some older girlfriends by then, kids 16 or so, and they were
having sex, so I decided to have it, too.*

*Then I moved in with my boyfriend. We both worked and
that's how we could afford an apartment. I lived with him for
two years, and I was taking the pill so I thought I couldn't get
pregnant. But I did.*

Josie, 17: *I had plenty of love when I was a kid. My parents were
great. They blame themselves, but it's not their fault. I just got
in with the wrong crowd. I got into sex much too early. We
didn't do drugs or alcohol, but sex was the thing.*

*I'd say to younger kids, stay away from sex if you can, but
if you can't, use protection. I made bad decisions. I decided to
have sex and I didn't protect myself, so here I am pregnant
and about to have a baby. I'm smart and I'm a good student,
but I sure wasn't smart about this.*

Joyce, 17: *You adults out there who want to change things just
can't do it for teens. They have to do it for themselves. I'm
still working on changing me. I want to be more positive. I
want to be the best mother I can be.*

*Positive peer pressure has to come from your peers, and
everybody wants to fit in. These days kids aren't listening to
their teachers or their parents, why would they listen to you
or to me?*

*I have three young cousins and I try to talk to them all the
time. One is 15 and she just lost her baby. But she wants
another one. They let the guys pressure them. One even has
an STD. They don't believe they can get AIDS.*

*They worry me a lot and I try to do everything I can to get
them to listen to me, but they don't. They hate preaching just
like I did. When they go through something real negative, then
they'll believe it, but they have to find out themselves.*

Are the Pregnancies Intentional?

Some people say teens have babies because they want to.
Dash supports this,[24] as does Bea Moran, a social worker at an
alternative high school in Bradenton, Florida. She says there are
some accidents, but she thinks a lot of it is intentional, a way for
them to see themselves differently because they don't like what
they've been seeing.[25] While we can't determine their deepest
motivations, we can listen to their words.

Sarah, 16: *I chose to have a baby because my dad came home
and wanted to take my twin sister and me to the North where
he lived, and I thought if I got pregnant he wouldn't be able to
take me.*

*He could, I guess, but he doesn't want to now because he
thinks it's better for me to stay with my boyfriend. So I'm
living with Mom.*

*She's alone without us, so she's glad to have me. At first
she was sad that I was pregnant, but then she said there was
nothing we could do and we had to cope. She works, and
we're looking for a home for us. Now we're getting excited.*

Shawn, 16: *I wanted this child. I planned it. I was living with my
dad, and I was lonely because he was drinking hard. My
boyfriend told me he had been told he couldn't have children
and he thought I'd leave him because of that. So I set out to
prove to him that I wouldn't leave him, and I got pregnant.*

*I wanted this child for another reason, too. I wanted a
child because it mattered to me to have someone to love the
way I love her.*

Rhonda, 17: *I chose to get pregnant. I wanted a baby, so I slept
with a guy. Two weeks later I changed my mind, but it was too
late. I never considered adoption. I felt it was my responsibility to keep her. I'm glad I did because I love her very much.*

Sometimes I do worry about the fact that I am so young,

and I worry about losing control. Now that she talks some it's getting better because she can tell me what she wants instead of screaming so much.

I wanted to get pregnant because I was so lonely. My mom worked and there was no one at home. After work she went to bars. So at 14 I found a man. I was sure he was "the one." He was my first love, the first man I ever slept with. Now that he's a dad he's a deadbeat. He never calls or visits, and he owes me child support.

Lonely, to keep a man, to avoid a move — these were the reasons given by these three teens. Dash catalogues the data that teens overwhelmingly wanted to have their babies, and had sex with this intent.[26] Most of the teens I interviewed told me they did not plan to become pregnant. Only three of the fifty said pregnancy was intentional.

According to *Sex and America's Teenagers,* 15 percent choose to have a child.[27] This may be closer to the reality. Schilling feels that a lot of teens don't know for sure. They may have fleeting moments when they think it could work. They may fantasize about a beautiful baby to hold, to be needed and loved by, to love. While many may know their consensual sexual activities may result in pregnancy, they are ambivalent, so do not actively prevent conception.

Schilling thinks, from his many conversations with those working with teen parents, that some teens may entertain these thoughts. He calls this marginal intentionality.[28] Some have naive romantic images that beginning a family might be feasible. Those girls with this marginal intentionality consider the possibility of becoming pregnant and bearing a child, and decide it would not be disastrous.

This is an important area for further research because of its potential impact on early intervention.

Other Factors

Still other factors, one societal and two developmental, are given by researchers and professionals focusing on adolescents:

- The fact that our society is laden with sexual symbols, in the media and in the real world as well, surely sets the tone, especially for poor teens who don't have opportunities to do other things to give them satisfaction.[29]

- As we continue to make progress in science, medicine and nutrition, the age of onset of menarche continues to decrease, typically at age 12 in 1988 compared with age 15 in 1890.[30]

- Learning disabled students, whose reading and writing skills are not sufficiently developed to be successful in school, are more apt to become teen mothers than are their academically successful peers.[31] Perhaps blocked success in one aspect of life may lead them to think they can at least succeed at motherhood.

Summary

How, then, do we answer the question at the beginning of this chapter, "What **are** they doing having sex so young?" When I talked with some of the concerned and/or angry adults asking this question, I heard other questions and comments.

"They're too young, for heaven's sake. They're inexperienced. They don't know how to take care of a baby."

"They think they're playing with dolls. They're ruining their lives, and their babies'."

"They have no morals. They're selfish. They're using up all the taxpayers' money."

"They only care about sex. They're lazy."

"They just want a baby to play with. They want a baby to love them."

"They think it's just their business, not ours, but we're paying for them."

"Why don't they want the father around? Why don't they get married? Where are their standards? Where are their values?"

"What's the matter with the home, the school, the church? Where's the discipline? What's wrong with marriage?"

"What's going to happen when all their babies become teenagers themselves? "

One 60-year-old retiree, traveling south, spent some time in an emergency ward in a rural town. She was sitting beside a 13-year-old mother holding her child. "They were both sucking their thumbs!" she told me, her tone a combination of bewilderment, annoyance, and compassion.[32]

Because everyone has an opinion on why teens are having sex too early, it's difficult to get a consensus. Are they "bad" girls? They are having sex outside of marriage, and for one-third of the adult population in this country, that is considered immoral. The majority of adults, however, although they feel that sexual intercourse is a healthy part of life, worry about teen sex because of HIV infection and other sexually transmitted diseases, and the cost to society of young mothers who can't afford to provide for their babies.[33]

The reality of unwed teen motherhood is that if these teen mothers are "bad," then the adult, unmarried female population is bad as well.[34] Teen unwed birthrates reflect the adult unmarried birthrate. Statistics on births to unmarried adults suggest to us that adults think that marriage may not matter. Unwed teen birthrates reflect the same thinking.

Are teens having sex earlier? Yes, they are. The age of first sex has decreased, according to all the studies. Among children born in the decade of the 30s, 43 percent of males and 32 percent of females had sex before age 18. By the 60s, 61 percent of males and 58 percent of females had sex before age 18, a 16

percent increase for males and a 26 percent increase for females.[35]

Are more teens having babies? Kristin Moore, Child Trends,
Inc., reports that despite a rise in the 80s, the teen birthrate is
lower now than it was in the 60s. What is higher is the number of
unmarried teens having babies.[36] The reality is that while there
are more children being born to single mothers, most of them are
adults, not teens. Seven out of every ten single mother births are
to women 20 years of age and older.[37, 38]

Are they choosing to have early sex, and are they choosing to
have babies? In spite of the tendency to blame the victim, it's
hard to blame a teenager who is sexually abused, perhaps raped
by a member of the family, mother's boyfriend, a family friend,
or an older stranger. In cases of early sexual abuse, followed by
consensual teenage sex, the data tells us that these teens are far
more likely than most to engage in early sex. Their self-esteem is
diminished; they may feel worthless except for sex. When teens
have sex with older men, they have either fallen victim to male
predators, or in their immaturity and inexperience they have
sought the security of a man who they think will take care of
them and take them away from their environment. Not too much
choice there, either.

But what of the teen who has consensual sex with another
teen? This sounds more like choice though we, being adults,
cannot know the full power of peer pressure and societal
pressure to conform to the sexual mores of this decade.

What of the teen who says, "I wanted a child"? Surely there is
a choice being made here. Yes, there are some who say this, and
I think they mean it. But nearly every teen mother I spoke to —
whether she said she got pregnant intentionally or not — felt she
was much too young to be a mother and wished she had waited.

Second and third births to unmarried teens indicate that this
may be the area in which real choice is made. However, a more

likely alternative to this thinking is that the same factors that induced early sex and early pregnancy may still be at work with teens for whom there has been no successful intervention.

My personal belief is that, whatever the reasons, early sex is not a good thing for these young women because they are not emotionally mature. Early pregnancy is even worse because it interrupts their education and causes them more stress than they are equipped to handle. It forces adult responsibilities on them when they are not adults.

Single parenthood compounds the problems. The poverty they have been reared in will follow them and their children. For many, the pattern will continue.[39] Their children are likely to become teenage parents, even as their grandmothers may have been. None of this is good for society, either. Only a public policy that deals with the large issues — poverty, education, joblessness, human sexuality — in a realistic and effective manner can change this pattern.[40]

Pragmatic programs, honest assessments of the problems of poverty, a re-establishment of a society that values children and cares for them — these are the routes to change. Though we cannot agree on the reasons, we do agree there's a problem. That's a big step toward agreeing on the solution.

3

Their Feelings About Men

This topic was the one, next to their desire to be good mothers, that inspired the most emotional discussions. The girls who were noisy and confrontational in the groups said that men were liars, cheats, phonies. They made promises they didn't keep, they led the girls on, they couldn't be trusted. The few quiet ones were those whose babies' fathers were still with them and were supportive. I think they were embarrassed to say good things about the men in their lives because of the overwhelming number in the group who were alone.

Effects of Sexual Abuse

They talked, too, about men as their partners, about their own fathers and stepfathers, and many talked about the sexual abuse they had been subjected to in their homes. They frequently said

they'd rather raise their children alone than have them go
through what they themselves went through with the men in
their lives.

In *Young, Poor and Pregnant,* Musick tells us that the trauma
caused by sexual victimization distorts a child's self-concept,
which then colors her future interactions with men.[1]

It's one thing to read it in Musick; it's another to hear it from
the teens themselves:

Marina, 15:

I Hear a Noise in the Night

I lie awake. My feelings are caught up in my head.
I pray for help but know there is no one,
No one to listen, no one to understand,
No one to talk to and no one to hear me.
My mind is running in circles. My head is spinning.
A noise at my door and I yell,
Please leave me in peace.
Please leave me alone in the night.

Karen, 18: *My sisters and I never told my mom about our
stepfather coming into our room and abusing us because we
were afraid of him. We just put up with it and tried to live as
best we could, but it was hard. I used to lie in bed and worry
about when he would come.*

*Finally, when I was ten, Mom found out, and she took off
her wedding ring and threw him out. I was so happy that she
loved us better than him, and I think she's a great lady for
doing that.*

*I'll never get another man into this house, that's for sure.
But I have to find some men for my son to know. He'll need to
interact with a male — maybe through school and through
sports. The one thing I promise myself is that he'll never have
to be afraid like I was.*

Rosalyn, 23:

Abuse

Dark silhouette in the doorway
Babysitter's son
No question asked, deed begun.
A taste of what's to come.
In bed, legs spread,
Small child's fears
Tall boy, not yet man,
Listens to the tears.
Doesn't care . . . all the same
Ten years later, won't remember name.
But I do. The deed done
Was forgotten with the rising sun. Or was it?

I was two when my parents were divorced. I lived with my mother. I was sexually abused by the babysitter's son when I was 7. It colored my thinking about men and I've never felt secure about my relationships with guys since then.

Then, at eighteen, my father wanted me to come live with him. I thought it was time to get to know my father. He was blind and he lived with a man who took care of him. Dad thought it was up to him to educate his daughters about sexuality, and he told me that was one way he could get to know me. But I felt disgusted when my father put his hands on me. It felt wrong. I told him, "No way." He listened to me but I still couldn't stay.

Marianne, 16: *I worry about guys. I was raped three times by people I knew. I don't want to be molested again. They think sex is love. They say they'll be with you forever. But they don't really love you. My baby really loves me. I do love her, and I also love my mom no matter what I may say about her. I'll be there always for both my child and my mom.*

Lenore, 21: *My father abused me sexually for years, even after I became a mother and moved back into my parents' home when my daughter was small. But when the abuse continued, and I began to fear for my child as well as for myself, I moved out and took him to court. The family, including my grandparents, became angry with me and threatened me with bodily harm if I didn't drop the charges, so I did. But I can't drop the memories the way I dropped the charges.*

I haven't been able to recall every face that goes with every name in all of the interviews I did, but I see Marina, Marianne, Rosalyn, Karen, and Lenore each time I reread their stories. Each tried to tell me about her experience in an objective way, to talk about it as if it were someone else. But if their voices didn't betray their feelings, their body language did. They looked away, they tensed their bodies, they pursed their mouths — yet they kept talking, wanting me to hear about their abuse. Perhaps talking about it helped them to put it aside. Or maybe they thought the world should hear it.

While I was listening, I thought about myself, my own daughter as a little girl and my granddaughters as they are now, and I found my own body reacting like theirs. Could these things really happen to young girls? Are these stories isolated cases, even unusual? Unfortunately, they are not, say the researchers.

Debra Boyer conducted a study in the state of Washington, which concluded that 62 percent of the teen mothers interviewed had been sexually abused. Victims averaged 10 years old; their abusers, often adult male family members, averaged 27 years old.[2] The unthinkable is real.

"He Said He Loved Me"

When we think of sexual abuse we think of force and violence. We also know that all teenage sex is not rape, and we know that physical abuse isn't always a partner to intercourse.

Let's look at other pressures, pressures that are less physical and more psychological. What about the pressures that poor young women feel to be loved, to fill a void in their lives, to be part of a family or to escape the lives of poverty that they are living?

What about peer pressure to conform? Teens, ages 15 to 17, talk about these pressures.

Alice, 15:

Love is a Sensation

Love is a sensation
Caused by a temptation
When a boy sticks his temptation
Into your combination
It increases the population.
Hugging is a pleasure
Kissing is a shame
Guys get all the pleasure
Girls get all the pain.
When they say they love you,
You think it's true,
When your stomach starts to grow,
They say the hell with you.
So is sixty minutes of pleasure worth nine months of pain?
Three days in the hospital and a baby without a last name?
So they say when they meet you, I like you.
When I like you, I love you.
When I loved you, I let you.
I let you and I LOST you!

Marina, 15: *The area we lived in was bad, you know, drugs, liquor, bad people hanging around. It was hard to be good in such a bad place, and I know I shouldn't have fallen for the*

*old line that he loved me and he would always love me. They
sweet talk to get you, and then everything changes when you
get pregnant. They forget all the hugs and kisses and nice
words, and they leave you for someone who's not pregnant
and who still wants to play with them.*

*My boyfriend was a fatal attraction. He'd been my boy-
friend since second grade. He bought me stuff. He was nice to
me. But he isn't any more. You find these things out for
yourself. Nobody can tell you.*

Gail, 17: *He's gone and good riddance. He left right after my
daughter was born, and now he's doing coke. I can't find him,
but the truth is I don't really want to. I'm off of drugs and I'm
taking good care of my daughter. I'm working hard at school,
too, and I don't need a guy around to make trouble for us.*

*I started having sex when I was 12, on a dare. My best
friend dared me to do it with her boyfriend, and I did. But
now I only have sex if I really care about someone, and only
after he's been checked for HIV.*

The research backs up these stories. Musick explains that poor
adolescent girls lack self-esteem and are psychologically vulnerable. Without social and economic support, they will find it very
hard to resist potentially harmful behaviors which promise to
satisfy unfulfilled longings and to make up for past hurts. These
young women are at considerable risk for exploitation and early
initiation of sexual activity.[3] Sadly for themselves and for
society, these new experiences reinforce their poor self-image.
Once again, they are failures in their relationships with men.

Violence Is Increasing

Just as psychological abuse leaves young women with emotional trauma, so, too, does physical abuse. Males cites the
teenage violent crime statistics — over the last decade murder is

up 50 percent, and violent crime arrests among adolescents have doubled. Poverty sets the stage, and adult crime rates write the script for the adolescent actors who follow the mores of the times. Males goes on to say that violence, mostly by adult parents and caretakers, kills 1,000 children and seriously injures 140,000 more a year.[4]

This teen's story reflects the climate of violence she was raised in, and supports the predictions of researchers about how these teens will behave:

Diana, 17: *I met the baby's father in a drug program. He was clean and sober by then, and seemed great. He was sweet to me, nice. I felt so good. Then he got emotionally abusive and got into heavier and heavier drugs. He'd been so good to me I felt that I was born to help him. I knew I loved him, and I'd do anything for him.*

When I had our baby I thought he'd straighten out, but he didn't. He ran away from the drug program, got jailed for breaking and entering, violated his probation, and now he's back in jail.

A participant in a workshop in a northern city summed it up. "My baby's dad is violent, so who needs him? When they beat you, you're better off alone."

Older Men as Predators

The "lucky" teen mothers, the ones who have not been forced or coerced into early sex, yet have suffered the psychological effects of poverty and neglect, tell their stories about their relationships with older men.[5] My sense of this phenomenon is that in many of these cases the men are "predators," men who attract young girls with their age, money, and what is perceived as sophistication, then use them and leave them. But in some cases it may be that a young girl sees the father figure she has been looking for, and reaches out to the older man to find the security and love she has been missing. In either case, most of these relationships do not last, and the teen mothers are left where they were before, deserted. Only now they have a baby.

Joyce, 17: *I was itchy. I was 14, I looked 16, and I thought he was younger than 30. He was a very attractive man. I had the baby, and then he got abusive. He started beating me up, and I just picked up my child and I left. I don't ever let him see my baby. I had to get a restraining order on him, but I still want child support and I'm going for it.*

He used to say that if he was going to take care of the baby, I had to be his girlfriend. But I'm not going to be his girlfriend ever, and I still am going to go for child support. I have a new friend now, but we don't have an intimate relationship because I'm just not ready for that. If I had a chance at a second life, I would have waited, but I don't, so I'm going to do the best I can.

Tameka, 18: *The baby's father probably doesn't know about my pregnancy. He's gone off to the Job Corps. I told his mom but*

I'm not sure she told him. I don't like to smoke and do drugs and hang out, so I'm better off without friends.

I do have one friend now, a good man. He's 28, and he's happy about my baby coming. He already has six kids who are with their mothers, and he doesn't get to see them. So he's excited about this baby. I am, too.

Jacqueline, 16: *I think about the baby's dad sometimes. That's a real long story. I was with him for a couple of months when I told him I was pregnant. He thought it was a joke, that I was just trying to get even because I had caught him with another girl. He's 22 and working, and finally he said if I needed help with money he'd be there. But I don't believe him, and I'd rather he had nothing to do with the baby anyhow.*

He's into drugs, partying. I knew that when I slept with him, but I was into that lifestyle then, too. When I got pregnant, I quit it all. I don't need him. I don't want him. I told him just because I thought he had a right to know. Now he has another girl pregnant.

They didn't see themselves as being coerced by the males, but when we look at the age differentials — the young women 14 to 18 and the men 22 to 30 — we have to wonder about the ability of a young teen to withstand the attention, sexual attraction, and the possibility of escape from poverty that they hope an older man might provide.

Rare cases? According to Guttmacher's *Sex and America's Teenagers*, in 1988 30 percent of teen mothers 15 and under and 21 percent of teen moms 18 and under were impregnated by males at least 6 years older.[6] Are these cases of coercion? While not violent, are they pressures of the psychological kind, programmed by the social and financial pressures of poverty?

Debra Boyer is succinct and insightful when she says, "There

is no curriculum written to give a 14-year-old the skills to deal
with a 20-year-old who wants to have sex with her."[7]

Neglect and Desertion

Teen mothers, when referring to men, speak of sins of omis-
sion as well as sins of commission. For them, neglect and
desertion by their fathers and their babies' fathers rank right
behind abuse. They feel a sense of rejection and loss. They
defend themselves by saying, "I don't care about men. I don't
want them in my life."

Fran, 18: *When I told him I was pregnant he said I was crazy,
that I was acting weird, and that he didn't believe me. I told
him he could leave, but he wouldn't. I was even mean to him
to get him to go, but he still stayed.*

*I thought about abortion and Mom really wanted it, but I
decided not to do it, and I'm so glad. My baby is seven
months now and he's terrific. The father is still around, but
not with us, and I'm glad about that, too. He visits sometimes,
but he doesn't help much with caretaking. He moves from job
to job, and when he has money, he gives us some.*

Helena, 17: *The dad isn't much. He stops by and says "Hi" to
his son. Big deal. He's not doing any fathering at all, but still
I think it's important for the baby to know he has a father. If
he'd get a job, stop hanging out with his friends, and pay a
little more attention to the baby, I might take him back, but
that's not going to happen. And I'm struggling enough as it is.
What do I need him for just to add to my troubles? If he has
nothing to give me, then he'd better get out of my face.*

*Right now I don't really care about men. I have to know
more about life and about men before I get into a relationship
again. And besides, I want to take up nursing or working with
kids, and that takes up too much time to have any left for men.*

Rosamund, 15: *My baby's father moved out of town to go live with his mother when I was seven months pregnant. The baby is 14 months old now, and he just came back to town. He wants her on weekends, but I don't give her to him. I don't have transportation to take her, and anyhow, I don't want him in my life.*

I have no boyfriends now. I don't want sex. I don't have any feelings about having a relationship with a boy at all.

When we hear the negative feelings these teen mothers have about men and then look at the mores of adult single women in our society, we begin to understand why marriage has no place in teens' plans. Nationally, the share of families headed by a single parent increased from 22 percent in 1985 to 26 percent in 1994.[8] Teens look around and see adult women, unmarried, with babies. Adult women account for a larger percentage of the out-of-wedlock births in the United States each year, having increased fourfold in the last twenty years.[9] In other words, teens see their own single mothers, sisters, and other single females in their lives, and they ask, "What's the point of getting married?"

Others ask, "Who needs men?" Like the female adult role models they emulate, they don't feel the need.

Risk of AIDS

But what about AIDS and other sexually transmitted diseases? The more cautious teens, and some who have been exposed to sex education, think about safe sex. Most young people, even those who think they don't have much to live for, are not ready to die. We're told that sexually experienced teens are doing a better and more consistent job in the use of contraception.[10] Those who use condoms are much less likely to contract an HIV infection or other STD. However, younger teen women, rarely prepared to protect themselves from either pregnancy or STDs, don't discover contraception until they have become pregnant.

Another strategy teens are adopting is a form of protection sometimes called "serial monogamy." This is based on public health advice that, to cut the risk of contracting a disease, sexually active teens have only one partner.[11] Unfortunately, unmarried people, young and old alike, often translate this advice into one partner *at a time*. "I won't be promiscuous," they think, "and I'll be safe." We know that this is a false assumption, for each new partner may have already been exposed to multiple partners, some of whom may be carrying the HIV virus.

Ellsbeth, 18: *My baby's dad? He likes to cheat. We don't get along. He's 18, but he acts a lot younger. He doesn't like to take care of the baby, and he doesn't like to work. He has a job, but he pays no money for her support. Now that he's 18, I'm taking him to court to collect child support.*

He gets violent sometimes. When I lived with him he used to hit me, but I'd known him since fifth grade and I thought I loved him.

I don't think about marriage at all. I don't want to be married just to break up. I can't see the advantage. You have all that paper work and legal problems, and anyhow, I don't care about men any more. I don't want any more children, and I don't care about sex, so I don't need a man in my life.

Tanya, 18: *The first dad and I split up, and I met the new guy who is the father of my two younger children. But he's in jail now, so we don't see him at all. The first dad comes around now and then to visit. He just comes in to play, and then he's gone. We're friends now, but not lovers.*

I'm not interested in sex with anyone now. One day, maybe, I might decide to get married, and then I'll think about if I want more kids. But right now I'm full-time busy.

Jewel, 17: *The baby's father really wanted to be part of her life, and even though I didn't want him, I knew it was important for her to have a father. He pays child support, and he sees her twice a week. He'd probably like to get married, but I don't want to.*

I don't want to have to put up with his, or any other guy's, crap. I don't want someone always asking me where am I going, what am I doing. I want to have my own life with my child. I'll work hard.

A teen in a group, echoing what she had been taught at home, said:

Momma said sex is going to happen in your life. She says it's better to be married, but it's a natural thing and it's not wrong. But she says you don't sleep around. Just one guy and that's it. I stick with one guy, and I don't carry my baby all around the place just to be with guys.

Positive Attitudes for Some

Are we to conclude, then, that all teens have been abused either sexually, physically, or psychologically, and that they all either fear men or are disappointed in them? Do all teen mothers hate their own father and/or the fathers of their children? No. There are also stories of loving dads and supportive partners who make a real difference in the nurturing of their children.

Another factor plays a role in teens making change and making it work. Even though many of these young women came from poverty, and even though some have been abused, they were resilient enough to come through it with healthy attitudes.[12]

Anne, 21: *I find I love my dad now, and I especially enjoy the attention he gives Robbie. They are very close which is good because Dad is the male role model a six-year-old needs. There are no other good men in our lives because I have no*

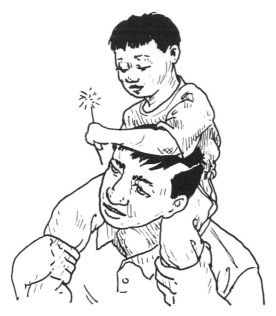

interest in dating at all. Maybe someday when my son is grown up, but not now.

Robbie does see his dad every other weekend so I don't have to tell him much about his father. He can find out for himself. His dad didn't come through when we needed him, but I guess it's good for Robbie to see him and know he has a father.

Bobbie, 16: *The baby's dad is seventeen and he's working. But even so, he's worried. Mainly about money. He's from another country and he isn't in school, but he makes lawn furniture and works very hard, sometimes ten hours a day. When he comes home, he cleans and cooks. So I'm lucky because he's a good man. We still like each other, and we hated to say good-bye every night, so now we live with his brother and his wife. We split the bills. His parents and mine give us some money to help.*

Brenda, 16: *If I could turn the clock back, I'd stay a virgin and not even have sex until I was in college. I'd just wait until I was old enough to not want to be a kid anymore because one mistake, and that's your WHOLE life.*

My baby's dad is only 15. He's around on his day off, but

*he has no money. He's still a boy, and I'm a woman. He
doesn't go to school a lot.*

*My mom says I can do better, but I don't want another
boyfriend and I don't want to be alone, so I just stick with
him. I'm not getting married. He's neat with the baby, though.
He talks to him, he holds him, he shows him he loves him. I
don't want to think about men for a while, except to stay
friends with the dad. I think my hormones have changed since
I had a baby. I'm not interested.*

Shunika, 18: *The first time I remember my father really talking
to me was the year I entered seventh grade and got up the
courage to ask him for a snowmobile for Christmas. He
mumbled something I couldn't hear and went into the garage
to work on one of his old cars. My younger brother and I had
always been afraid of him because he was so grim and silent,
and we stayed out of his way as much as we could.*

*Christmas morning finally came and I went to look under
the tree without much enthusiasm. There was a large package
for me, but certainly not big enough to be a snowmobile, so I
opened it with my usual lack of interest.*

*"To Shunika," the card inside read. "Here are the small
parts. The chassis is outside. If you want to learn to ride it,
you have to know how to put it together. Love, Dad."*

*I screamed with excitement, hugged him, and we began to
talk about our plans for putting it together. I understand now
that he could only talk to me about what he knew, and that
was mechanics.*

Shawn, 16: *I am still with my boyfriend and we live together.
He's 25, works two full-time jobs to support us. He is a nice
man. He makes sure I have what I want and the baby has
what she needs. He's unselfish with both of us. He loves her
as I do, but he's not crazy about taking care of her, you know,*

diapering and that kind of stuff. But he works hard to take
care of us, and that's okay with me.

Life is good now, except that I worry a little because he's
on probation for a DUI. But he's stopped drinking, and I
think he's going to keep it up. We have some problems, but we
get along really well most of the time. One day we plan to
marry.

Tracy, 16: *When Mom first got divorced, we lived with my*
grandparents for six years till we got our own place two years
ago. So I had no father, but my grandfather is a good man.
He's okay with my being pregnant, and worries more about
my well-being than about anything else. He was a preacher,
and he's mellowed out a lot since he got older.

Dad is still my father even though I don't talk to him. I just
wish he'd be happy for me that I have someone to love who
will love me back.

The baby's father loves me to death and I love him back.
He never hits me, he never degrades me, he's generous, he's
mellow, he ups my self-esteem. I overreact a lot, I have a bad
temper, I do stupid things, and he knows just what to do to
make me calm. He's my rescuer, my life saver.

In spite of teen mother protestations that they don't want or
need men in their lives, in spite of the adult and teen women who
decry marriage and opt for single parenthood, we know that
good fathers make a big difference in the lives of children. They
are needed by both the mothers and the children.

Studies describe how the support of a male partner plays a
critical role in affecting teen mothers' behavior toward their
children. Their sense of being supported makes a difference. It
helps them feel less anxious and reduces caregiving stress if they
feel the emotional support of a man.[13]

As for daughters, the presence of a supportive father can

make the crucial difference in the daughter's self-image. Mary Pipher, author of *Reviving Ophelia: Saving the Souls of Adolescent Girls,* studied this relationship and concluded that fathers can model good male-female relationships and respect for women in a wide variety of roles. Fathers can teach their daughters that it's safe to be smart and independent. Emotionally available fathers can help produce daughters who have high self-esteem, a sense of well-being, and a confidence in their relationships with men.[14]

The teens whose stories reflected lack of self-esteem and emotional trauma about men drew me back once again to my own adolescence. Where was my self-esteem and confidence in relationships with boys when I was in high school? Where was my self-esteem and confidence when I married at 21? Nowhere that I could find. In my otherwise all-female family, my own father was too ill and too self-involved to provide the role model and the relationship Dr. Musick discusses.

I got lucky, once again, this time by marrying a man who supplied both for me. And, along the way, I worked with several men who taught me that's it's okay to be independent. We could still be friends. What about these young women whose fathers and whose babies' fathers provided none of this? Where will they go from here?

Summary

We heard how the majority of teen mothers feel about men. What does this say to us, the adults who, unless we provide the necessary intervention, will be faced with the reality of babies who become teenagers and have babies themselves? There are as many feelings as there are histories, but some overriding themes were encountered over and over as teens related their experiences.

Their fathers — their first male role models — could have been very important in their development. Unfortunately, most of them weren't home when the teens were growing up. Their single mothers may have had a man in the home, but he usually wasn't the father. If fathers were home and not abusive, they were emotionally distant. Anger, distrust, and sometimes fear color these young moms' relationships with men as they approach womanhood. If they were abandoned, the teens harbor deep feelings of loneliness, rejection, and jealousy.

Frequently, fathers left home to form new relationships with women, and deserted the children of their first marriage for the children of their second or third. Fathers who were not positive role models because of their absence or negative behavior delayed the social and sexual development of their daughters. These young women were likely to approach their own developing sexuality with little idea of the qualities to look for in a man when they began to think about men, or what qualities to recognize in a man when men began to think about them.

Those initiated into too-early sex, violent or otherwise, were easily persuaded by peers or seduced by older men, and found themselves teen mothers. Ambivalent about this role, but socialized to believe that keeping their babies was the right thing to do, they became teen mothers when they were psychologically unprepared for motherhood.

The younger fathers, little more than boys themselves, were unprepared for the responsibility of fatherhood and unable to provide financial or emotional support. Older males, frequently the fathers of other children and not committed to fathering this child, generally deserted the mother both emotionally and financially. Child support was absent in most cases, so the cycle of poverty continued for these teens and their children.

Deserted again, still poor, and now responsible for a child, these teen mothers see very little hope in their lives.

I interviewed white, African American, Hispanic, and Native American girls and young women, and the feelings were the same. The contributing factors were poverty, abuse, neglect, and abandonment; the results were early sex and early motherhood; and the feelings teens harbored were anger, fear for their children's safety, disappointment, and sadness. Who cares? Who needs men? echoed in their stories.

When there were good men in their lives, and when the young women were personally strong enough and/or had been raised by strong enough women and/or involved in good social programs, the teen mothers were "making it."

The implications for society here are both frightening and exciting. It is critical that we spend as much time and energy on young men as we do on young women. Boys need to understand about sex and its consequences, well beyond what the media and the streets teach them, and what they see modeled by many of the men in their lives. They need to know that their role in childrearing is as important as the mothers'. They need to know that they can gain satisfaction from being good fathers well beyond the current stereotype that a boy who fathers a child is now a man.

Those who become young fathers need to be involved in caretaking roles from the beginning, giving them the same opportunity to bond with their babies as the mothers have. Older males need to be convinced that neither society nor the law will condone their taking advantage of young girls or of shirking their fathering responsibilities when they create children.

Think about the possibilities we might open up to the current generation of preteens if they were able to have the necessary mentors and education in their lives that are now missing.

The Meaning
of Motherhood

When I asked teen moms to talk to me about being mothers and raising children, they drew on their own experiences. They recalled the poverty, the frequently absent or abusive fathers, and the single, sometimes abusive, often exhausted mothers. They talked about the neglect, the inconsistent parenting, the drug use, crime, violence, and the lack of opportunity in their lives.

The few who had warm, devoted mothers nevertheless succumbed to peer pressure or were seduced by adult males and found themselves teen mothers. Many had sex too early and were parents too young. They realized things had gone wrong for them. Could they make it right for their children? Could they be good mothers? That's what they wanted most, they told me.

Judith Musick, a developmental psychologist, describes her

research on this topic in *Young, Poor, and Pregnant.* She writes
about the realities of being a young mother, yet she expresses
hope for their futures and the futures of their children. There are
different meanings in being a teen mother than in being an older
mother. The teen, too young and still too close to her problems
with her own mother to have been able to resolve them, may
project these issues onto her child. She may unconsciously
expect the child to be the main provider of her love. She may not
be able to separate her child's needs from her own. Dr. Musick
has a wonderful quote from a teen who, when asked why her
child wasn't wearing a jacket on a winter's day, said, "I'm
not cold."[1]

What parent can't relate to that? The teen's inability to
individuate her child from herself, her immaturity, lack of
knowledge about child development, and difficult life circumstances combine with her personal experiences to determine the
kind of mother she will be.

But change is possible. Teen mothers grow up to become
older mothers. Maturity brings distance; experience brings
growth. External, professional guidance can teach the skills
needed to make the changes. The really good news is that the
most significant predictor of improved parenting depends on the
teen's desire to change and her willingness to seek and use help.[2]
Teens I spoke with expressed that desire.

In the interviews that follow, the moms recognize that they
missed the closeness, the attention, the nurturing, the "being
there" they felt they needed. They'll provide it for their children,
they said.

Shunika, 18: *A little kid is like a seed. It needs to be watered,
talked to, and nurtured. If that happens, it will grow to be a
strong plant, able to get along no matter what the obstacles. It
may need some watering beyond the rain once in awhile, but*

mostly it will be independent and successful on its own. But if it grows without knowing it's loved or being told it's lovely, it will be stunted and lack the drive to succeed.

If some loving gardener comes along and begins to tend it carefully, it will come back to something like it should have been, but it will always need attention and encouragement to keep going. And the caretaker who most matters with that little kid is, I believe, the mom.

Shawn, 16: *It's hard, sure, and I miss my friends and the fun we used to have together. But I can't do all that and be a mother, too, so I made my choice. I'd do anything, give up anything, for my baby.*

I told her father, too. If I have to choose between you and my child, it's going to be my child. When I look at this little girl now, and when I hold her, and when she stops crying, smiles, and reaches for me, it's all worth it. She knows I'm her mom, and I sure know it, too.

Alana, 15: *My baby's father and I talk a lot about how we want to raise this child. We want her to be smart, to be educated, to be active and athletic, and to become someone. We don't want her to have children until she's old enough and she's ready. I'll talk to her. I'll tell her what happened to me. I'll explain it all to her. I'll tell her she can talk to me and I'll listen. I'll teach her how to protect herself. I'll be close to her, not like my mom and me. Even though we talk to each other now, we're not that close.*

Tameka, 18: *I'm not really close to my mom, but I am close to my grandparents. I lived with them most of my life. Grandma is like a mom to me. She cooked, she took care of me, she's concerned for me. She's helpful. She advises me and we talk a lot. She listens. She gives her opinions, but she doesn't come down hard. I want to be that kind of mom.*

Following Through on Promises

Helena and Diana remember insecurity. They never felt safe because the rules kept changing. They'll make sure they're consistent, they'll follow through on promises, and above all, they'll be honest:

Helena, 17: *I'll raise this baby totally different from the way I was raised. I want to set rules. I want him to have everything he needs and to feel really special, and I want him to know that I love him, but that I'm the momma and he needs to listen to me.*

I want to be his friend, but I want to be more than his friend. And I won't forget promises I make like my mom did and still does with me. I'm going to say if I can, I will. And if I say I will for sure, then I really will.

I know I won't fight in front of my child, and I won't keep secrets from him either. When my parents split, I thought it was my fault. Nobody ever told me different. I'll make sure my son knows that not having a father wasn't his fault.

Diana, 17: *I think I'll be a good mother because I get it when people talk to me now. I hear dishonesty, and I hear someone saying they need help. Maybe all the bad stuff that happened to me finally got through. I'll do everything I can to make it good for him.*

Will the Poverty Continue?

We must think that, if we provide the right kinds of education and motivation, it's possible to change behavior. If we didn't believe this, would there be so many teachers, social workers, therapists, motivational speakers, and religious leaders?

But do we believe we can change poverty, the strongest predictor of teen pregnancy and motherhood?[3] More than 80 percent of teen mothers were living in poverty before they became pregnant.[4] Now, in addition to their own needs, they have a child to provide for. Will they be able to provide both the material and the psychological sustenance needed to be good mothers?

These teens believe they will, even though the data tells us that unmarried teen mothers are less likely to finish high school,[5] will, by prime working age, have half the median personal income of those who graduate,[6] and their children are more likely to spend their childhoods in poverty.[7] We're told that this combination of less education, fewer job opportunities, and possibly becoming dependent on welfare[8] will combine to perpetuate the cycle so that their children are more likely to become teen parents themselves.[9] Yet, in spite of all the difficulties, these teens are optimistic and believe that they can make the necessary changes to escape the route that poverty has mapped out for them.

Ellsbeth, 18: *I want my son to be strong, well-balanced, stable, to be able to talk about his problems and to be able to listen when someone else is talking to him. I want him to be able to take care of himself, to be able to keep house, to cook, to not be a couch potato and expect the world to take care of him. I worry about his being near or seeing violent behavior, and I worry about bringing him up in a world with so much hate and with so many wars. I want him to know peace and harmony, and to be healthy.*

Brenda, 16: *Mom is always telling me, my sisters, and my brothers how much she loves us. She is always hugging and kissing us. But she says it's very hard. There's never enough of anything, not enough time, or money, or energy. And there are always bills to pay. But she made it work for us just the same.*

Take Christmas, for instance. One Christmas when she had

no money at all she went to the Salvation Army and signed up
for free toys. She wrapped them up somehow and made it a
real Christmas even though we were dead broke. And Christ-
mas is still big in our house. Every year all the family comes
home and they bring all their friends. When we have money
we have turkey and ham, rice and beans, and Grandma's old
recipes. It's great and I'm glad we have this tradition for
my baby.

Education Seen as a Way Out

The teen mothers who sounded most convincing to me, those
who sounded most able to make the necessary changes in their
lives so that their children will be happy and well adjusted —
these were the young women who talked about getting an education, for themselves and for their children. They realized that
education is the way out of whatever ghetto you happen to be in.

These teens also realize what a wonderful job their alternative
schools are doing in providing good education, nurturing, and
positive role modeling for them.

Gail, 17: *If I could have a whole different life up to now, I'd*
choose it. But I can't, and I learned from my mistakes. I think
God had a part in it, too. If He'd wanted a different path for
me, He'd have chosen it. But I'm glad He chose for me to be a
mother. I'll see to it that my daughter isn't raised in a bad
place, that she gets to go to school.

I'll finish here and go on to Tech to become an accountant.
Then I'll get a good job and take care of her. I'm getting
there. It's hard, but they're really helping me, and I think I'll
make it.

Ginger, 13: *I want my baby to be educated, to go to college, to*
be the best she can be. I'll try to prevent her from getting
pregnant young, I'll teach her about birth control, I'll get her

the pill. I won't introduce her to sex, but I'll make sure she knows about it, and how to protect herself from pregnancy and from AIDS. I'm going to be the best mother I can be.

Tina, 17: *I'm doing okay. I feel good about my nine-month-old daughter and good about myself. If you don't feel good about yourself you can't feel good about anything you're doing. I'm raising my child in a happy environment. She's feisty. She's cute. She's like me and her father.*

My baby's father and I are together. He's a good person and a good dad. He's eighteen.

I don't feel I'm too young to have a child. I was happy when I got pregnant, and I'm happy now. He supports us, and we have an apartment with two other roommates. I'm finishing high school, and then I'm going on to get trained as a secretary. Now that I'm a mother, I have to do that so I can get a real job and be able to give her the things she needs. We're doing okay.

Shawn, 16: *I'm not kidding myself. I know it's hard to raise a child when you're as young as I am. There are 107 kids in this school trying to finish high school, and only about ten of them are still with their baby's dad. It's hard to work out that relationship, to stay in school, to raise a child, and a lot of us work, too.*

Does Past Abuse Affect Mothering?

Does a history of abuse affect teen mothering? Can this pattern be changed? Can young mothers learn the childrearing skills they need to replace the physical force they experienced?

Males, author of *The Scapegoat Generation,* tells us that family training is the genesis of violence. Children who are violently and sexually abused are three times more likely than non-abused youths to behave violently themselves.[10] In *Dubious Conceptions,* Kristin Luker confirms that babies of teenagers are more likely to be abused and neglected by their mothers than are babies of older mothers.[11]

Mindy and Rhonda worry about getting out of control. Since they don't have a lot of parenting skills, and the only model they've seen is in their own home where parents resorted to physical abuse, they are afraid they may hurt their children. They are trying to face up to their own emotional responses and are trying to learn from good role models. Will they be able to raise their children without being abusive even though abuse and neglect was a major part of their learning as children?

Mindy, 16: *I'm going along and seem to be doing okay, but when my daughter cries a lot, and I can't comfort her, I lose it again. It does an awful job on me. I want to be a good mother, and when I think I'm not, I feel like a failure.*

Rhonda, 17: *I live with my mom and my older sister and my two-and-a-half-year-old daughter. I have to live with Mom because I need her help financially. I don't think I could do it alone anyhow. It would be a lot of stress on me.*

My daughter drives me crazy. She screams when she wants her way, and I worry about getting out of control. I get mad and shake the crib, but I punch a pillow so I won't hit her.

I was never hit, but I did have alcoholic parents, and my father abused my mother by beating up on her. They were

*divorced when I was ten. I didn't think it had too much effect
on me, but maybe it did.*

*I want to be the best mother I can be. I see other mothers
doing it right, and I learn from that. I'm going to raise her
with self-esteem. She needs to feel good about herself. People
who don't feel good get into drugs and even suicide. I'll let
her know she's doing well, I'll praise her looks and her
behavior. I'm not going to be Susie Homemaker, but I'll be
there for her a lot more than my mom was for me. She won't
be raised in an alcoholic home or an abusive home.*

Some young mothers learned from good role models, too.
These had close, loving mothers or grandmothers, but still they
got pregnant young. Conditions of poverty, fatherless homes,
peer pressure got to them, and they're afraid it could happen
again with their children.

Joyce, 17: *I don't think I can do it all, no matter what I do
because my son will be what he wants to be. The mother of the
man I lived with is a great person, and she tried to raise her
son right, but he turned out to be very bad. My own mom was
a good lady, and she tried to encourage me, but I still did
what I wanted to do in spite of that. Peer pressure was just
too much for me.*

In *Motherless Daughters*, Hope Edelman describes adolescence as a period of intense internal chaos during which teens
see parents as oppressive and embarrassing. Most of adolescence, she says, is about allowing a new, more mature identity to
emerge from the cocoon of the family.[14]

But these teens, now mothers, don't have the liberty of
allowing time to create its maturational magic, so they come to
parenthood with their own mother conflict still fresh and hot.
Will they be able to take the giant step backward, assess their
own responses to their mothers whom they found authoritarian,

then take the giant step forward they need to be able to do it differently with their children?

"I hear my mother's voice coming out of my mouth, and it scares me," said a teen, talking in a group in the South. Heads nodded in agreement as the group discussed authoritarian, overprotective mothers.

Rosamund, 15: *It's kind of hard being a mother. At first I felt like she must be my mom's baby, not mine. I was too protective. I was afraid she'd be hurt and I couldn't help her. I watched her all the time. Then she got older, and she likes to be active and to play. She tries everything. She's talking. Suddenly it clicked in that she's growing up and I have to let her try on her own.*

Anne, 21: *I'm working on myself to let up and let go. When I realized how nervous I was, when I heard myself sounding like my mother, and when I saw my weight going up, up, up, I knew I needed counseling. So I go every week and think the counselor is really helping me.*

When we all lived together it was hard to raise Robbie because my mother was sure she knew the answers, and I was sure she didn't. But now that we live apart it's much easier. Robbie knows what I expect, I know what he needs, and we don't conflict.

Marina, 15: *You know the kind of book I'd like you to write? Write about how mothers should treat their kids. Write about when parents try to make things better for their kids but they make it worse. For instance, if Momma took over a problem I'm having with a friend, she'd make it worse. Kids have to do that themselves. Leave them alone.*

If parents bail you out all the time, you're not going to learn to be responsible for yourself. Leave them alone if you can and let them do it on their own. If they find out they can't do it, then come in and help. But make them responsible for themselves first.

Some teen mothers are still too insecure, too childlike to be good mothers. Musick agrees. She comments that because an adolescent mother is still something of a child, she is less able to modulate her impulses and emotions.[15]

Alana, 15: *I wouldn't do the same thing again if I could help it, even though I love my child, because I'm not ready emotionally. She takes up all of my time. She's active and won't let me do anything but play with her. She won't let me clean or shower or rest.*

I'm not ready financially. We're managing and I'm lucky her father is here, but I have to go to school and I have to learn how to earn a living. I just don't have time for what I have to do. I'll never be a kid again, and I'm only 15.

Brenda, 16: *My problems now are that I am always tired, I never have enough time or money, I can't go to movies or dances, and I miss being a kid. Now the biggest freedom I have is when the baby is sleeping and my work is done and I can just sit outside and rest. If he's sick I'm in worse trouble because then I can't go to work and the money is even less. I don't regret my baby. I love him and I'm glad I have him, but I wish I'd waited.*

Helena, 17: *My boyfriend left me just after I gave birth to our son. I was so worried. How can I be a father to my 9-month-old son when I don't even know how to be a mother? Having a baby is not a part-time job. It's full-time, and it's real. He needs all of me, and I need all of me just to be there for him. But I also have to go to school and I have to work, and then I'm supposed to do my homework and take care of my baby. There aren't enough hours in the day and I'm always tired.*

Others turn to God for comfort and guidance. Some have been raised by religious families and feel secure in their relationship to their God.

Some are questioning the beliefs they learned as young children. Others have exhausted their human contacts, and are reaching out for spiritual nourishment.

Ginger, 13: *My daughter is two months old now, and I'm really glad I have her. But I didn't always feel that way. I was only twelve years old and I didn't dare tell my mom. I waited 'til I was six months along, and then I had to tell her because I was really showing.*

We talked about abortion, but there was too much against it. I was too far along and it would have cost $2,000. We didn't have the money. Then I saw the baby on a sonogram, and I knew it was wrong to have an abortion.

When she was born I felt proud. She was mine and I didn't want to give her up. If God didn't want me to be a mother, it wouldn't have happened. I know I wouldn't give her up now for all the world.

Jewel, 17: *I depend on God to help me be a good mom. I'm Catholic and I go to church every Sunday. I believe someone is really, actually up there and that everything happens for the best.*

I think I'm a good person, and I'll raise a good child. But I know there isn't a lot I can do to help her if she's going to get into trouble. I know from experience. My mom tried to help me, and it didn't do any good.

Rosamund, 15: *I want to do a good job with my daughter. I'll talk to her about everything, and about sex, too. My mom never talked to me about sex, but I'll say to my daughter, "Don't get started too young. But if you do, come to me. I'll help you protect yourself. I'll get you the pill." I'd rather she* *told me and I'll be there for her.*

I was raised in the church, but I don't know what to think about her and church. If she wants to go, I'd never stop her. Sometimes I even go with my mom and take my baby with me. But still I'm not saved, and I go dancing. Some of the music is sexual, and I'm sure it's a bad influence, but I love to dance and I don't think it's bad for me or her.

Some of the younger teen moms were unrealistic, reaching for the moon. The childlike quality, the idealized sense of the possible, reminded me of Scarlett O'Hara in a scene from *Gone With the Wind.* Atlanta is sacked, Tara is in rubble, the fields are scorched, and Scarlett kneels to the ground, scratching for food. Finding nothing, she looks up and says, "I'll think about it tomorrow."

Some dream of sugar plum fairies, Brenda wishes she'd waited, Rosamund learns to let the reins out a little bit, Shunika tends her baby like a careful gardener, and Gail plans to become an accountant. Each is coping in her own way, trying to be a good mother.

"What really makes a good mother?" I asked myself.

Each teen recalls a different aspect of parenting that mattered to her and says, "Yes, that's it." What do we need to provide when we create earlier interventions for pregnancy prevention and support promising interventions for teen parents? What is the right mix? Is it staying home? Is it working? Is it juggling the two? Is the quantity of time spent with the child the ingredient that makes the difference? Is it the "quality time" we hear about? Or is the quality of the mothering the essence of the interaction between mother and child? Then I remembered, once again, my working mother, and I thought about myself as a six-year-old, on a bitter cold day in New England, and I wrote "The Needle."

The Needle
by Evelyn Lerman

I realize now that when I was six, the top of my head reaching just to the bottom of her ample breasts, she was 33. But then, standing in the clothing store beside her sewing machine, she was ageless. She was soft, she was hard, she was strong, she was mellow, and she smelled wonderful. She smelled of raised dough cinnamon buns and black coffee. Even today, when I smell cinnamon buns, no longer allowed because of cholesterol, I am transported back to the clothing store in Hyde Square, Jamaica Plain, Massachusetts.

The store itself smelled of clothing, and to my six-year-old eye it was wall-to-wall dresses, blouses, skirts, and an occasional man's suit. This was the place my mother went every day of the week except Sunday, the place where she earned a living. When people asked her how she earned a living, she would smile and answer, "With a needle." It was warm standing next to my mother, not only because she was hugging me, but because we were standing beside the pot bellied stove which she had stuffed with wood and lit at 5:00 that morning.

Before leaving for the store, she had prepared our breakfast,
left our father sleeping in his arthritic position in bed, and left us
with kisses and admonishments about dressing warmly and being
on time for school. Inspired by her energy and effort, we had
jumped out of bed, eaten, dressed, and walked in the 10-degree
cold to the store to say good-bye to our mother before going
to school.

So here I was, stuffed into my heavy jacket, gamely trying to
navigate in heavy winter boots, and wearing my warm, wool hat
with the pom-pom on top. This was the only piece of clothing
that felt right. It fit and it was warm, and the pom-pom was fun
to play with. We all kissed mother good-bye, and after she
supervised our safe crossing of Center Street, we took off in
different directions for our schools. I went to Wyman, the
elementary school for kindergarten through fifth grades. My
middle sister Blossom went down the street to Lowell, the
middle school for sixth through ninth graders. And my oldest
sister Miriam hopped the bus for the hour-long trip to Girls'
Latin School, where she had been sent because that was the way
to go to college.

I was sure to be late if I didn't hurry, so I tried to run all the
way to school. This was hard, first of all because I was so
heavily dressed, secondly because I was personally heavy, and
third because my legs and the rest of my body didn't work too
well together when the circumstance called for running. But I
tried, and made it just on time. What a joy it was to remove the
jacket and the boots, and then, finally, the hat.

As I slipped my fingers into the pom-pom, to give it one last
reassuring touch, I discovered a needle sticking up in the yarn. It
had to have attached itself to the pom-pom as I was being nestled
into my mother's bosom, for that was where she put her needles

when she was between sewing jobs at the store. She had pincushions in every size from small to large, but her bosom was her favorite place for needles until she was finished for the day. Here she kept the largest ones with the biggest eyes, and the smallest ones for the dainty jobs she also had to do.

I panicked! Would my mother need this needle to earn her living before the school day was over? I couldn't ask my teacher, Miss Dicey, because the first grade day was about to begin and it was not permitted to interrupt a class about something like a needle.

So I decided the best thing to do was hold it to make sure it wouldn't get lost. Since I am right handed, and I would need my hand to do things in school all day, I removed the needle from the hat with my left thumb and forefinger, and there I held it all day. I held it through classes in reading, I held it through recess, and I even held it while eating my sandwich during lunch. The long day finally ended. Clothed once again for the bitter cold, I took off for the store, and dutifully waited across the street until my mother spotted me so she could cross me to safety.

She gave me her usual warm smile combined with a crushing hug to her bosom, and I began to cry. "What's the matter, Babele?" she asked, using the Yiddish word for her youngest child.

"I was afraid to lose your needle," I sobbed.

Uncomprehending, she looked at me with a frown. "I don't understand."

I handed her the needle, my left hand by now nearly frozen in place, unaccustomed pains shooting up my arm. Between gulps of air I told her how I found the needle, how I worried she would need it, and how I saved it for her.

She beamed. "Babele, I love you. You are my life." She defined motherhood for me in many ways through her 75 years of life, but it was that moment, I am sure, that taught me what love looked like.

What was it about that moment that meant so much to me, so much that I remember it clearly 65 years later? As a little girl, it must have been the warmth of her hug and the love in her voice. When I think about it now, I realize it was all of that, but it was more. It was her total acceptance of me as her beloved child. Never mind that I hadn't thought of a smarter way to save the needle. Never mind that she would have understood if I threw it away. She loved the way I loved her, and she realized I had put her feelings first, before anything else that day would hold. Her selfless love for me had spilled over into my love for her.

That's the point, I think. We have to recognize these young women are really trying, trying to put their babies first, to make every day work in spite of the pain and the difficulty.

We, too, have to make every day count. We can't think about this tomorrow. We have to think about these mothers and their children today. We have to accept them, even if we don't think they made the wisest choice, and we have to be concerned about what happens to them. We have to be as concerned about those who have the courage to believe they can make it, as we are about the teens who are faltering, but still have hope.

We, like the teens, have to knock ourselves out in trying. We have to reach out, hug them, let them know we care, and by being good parents ourselves, show them how to be the good mothers they want to be.

The Worries
Come Swiftly

During interviews with teen mothers, they told me they
were worried. "What do you worry about?" I asked them. I had
expected them to be worried about their own lives. How were
they going to be kids themselves now that they had a child to
take care of? And though a few did express this concern, most
were worried about their children, and about their own roles with
their children. Their answers told me they worried because of
their own experiences. Many felt their own mothers hadn't really
"been there" for them, and they worried that they might not do a
good job with their own children.

In a survey of 45 teen mothers, 60 percent said they worried
about "doing a good job as a mother." Having come from lives
of poverty, 50 percent said they worried about "being able to
provide for my child." Again, reflecting their own upbringing,

50 percent worried about their children being affected by drugs, violence, and all forms of abuse. A few of the more mature teens, recognizing the problems of the larger world beyond their own neighborhoods, also worried about war and nuclear accidents, about "the world ending in my child's lifetime."[1]

Being a Good Mother

I wondered what they meant by "being a good mother" so I followed up with them individually. They spoke about things they knew. "Will I lose control and hit my child?"

"Will I be there for him/her?"

"Will I be able to stop her from having sex too young?"

"Will I be able to keep him safe from prejudice? He's bi-racial."

"Will I be able to provide her with a good education, and will I be able to complete my own education?"

"Will she have to go through what I have, with people hating me because I'm young and I'm a mother?"

Were they justified in their concerns, or were they paranoid about themselves and their children? The research tells us that they are more than justified when they worry about their own abilities to provide and protect.

In addition, their fears about their babies are real. Research shows that babies born to teenage mothers have more physical and cognitive problems than babies born to adult women.[2]

Brenda, Lenore, and Tracy are insecure about themselves and their role as mother:

Brenda, 16: *You know what I do worry about? I worry that my son will love his grandma better than he loves me because he spends so much more time with her and she is so good at it. When I first delivered him, I cried for two weeks because I couldn't do anything right for him. I touched him and he cried. I know that's because I was scared and he felt it. Now* *that I know what I'm doing he's happy with me, but I still worry that he'll want Grandma more than me.*

Lenore, 21: *Sometimes I think my daughter would be better off with a mother and father who could provide for her and care for her like real parents, not like me. I think it's because my mom always told me that I would never be a good mom.*

I feel like I'm a good mom, because I promised myself when I had her that I would love her unconditionally, and would never allow her to be hurt by me or anyone. She deserves a good life. She came into the world pure and doesn't deserve bad things happening to her.

Tracy, 16: *The baby's dad is 21. We're getting married when we can. He's working and paying for everything, even a private doctor. But still I'm afraid. I'm worried about the outlook of the whole thing. How will my father react?*

Who is at greatest risk for teen pregnancy? Among other variables, according to Katherine A. Kamiya, *Teen Pregnancy Summit Report,* are youth with low self-esteem and poor perceptions of their options . . . youth from single parent families and/ or without parental guidance or support.[3]

In *Reviving Ophelia,* Mary Pipher tells us that teenagers who are socially inadequate and lacking in confidence are the product of authoritarian parents who control too much and are too demanding.[4]

Finally, the American Association of School Administrators (AASA) points out in *Teenage Pregnancy* that a study in the Washington, D.C. metropolitan area found that the suicide rate of teen mothers is seven times higher than for other teenagers.[5]

These young women feel insecure for very good reasons. Their self-esteem will need a lot of building before they will gain the confidence they need to be the good mothers they want to be.

They Worry About Health

Jacqueline and Bobbie worry about their babies' health:

Jacqueline, 16: *I'm scared of being a mother at 16. It's a big thing. I'll have to learn how to deal with the ups and downs. And I'm worried, too. I feel lots of stress. Being pregnant made me grow up fast. Maybe too fast because I'm still a kid. But I can't be a kid now. I have to become a mother. And I worry about my baby. I want it to be healthy, so I have to put its needs before mine.*

I worry about money. Will I be able to support my baby? I'll have to get a job and get on my feet. My mom says she'll help me. She has a good job as an office manager and that's good, but she makes too much money for me to get much help from the government. I get WIC which is grocery money to buy milk, eggs, cheese, and juice so I can eat right while I'm pregnant. And I get temporary Medicaid for my care and for the delivery. But then I don't know what will happen.

Bobbie, 16: *I'm in the tenth grade and I'm doing well in school, but I'm worried, too. Will I be a good mother? Will I be able to take care of my baby? I'm accident prone is what they say.*

I'm worried whether the baby will be born okay. They say he's fine, but I still have the feeling that something's wrong. I'm very tired all the time. I've gained 35 pounds, and I feel heavy. I wasn't so thin before but I was in good health except for the bronchitis. I was born with bronchitis, and I've had it for most of my pregnancy.

I get very moody sometimes. I go from being scared to being happy. I'm confused, and all the time I'm tired and feel sick.

AASA indicates in *Teenage Pregnancy* that there is cause to worry. The United States has one of the highest rates of infant mortality of any industrialized nation. Twenty-five percent of low birthweight babies who survive their first year are at risk of being permanently disabled mentally and/or physically. Children born to teenage parents are significantly more likely to face difficulties when they reach school age. These children are at greater risk of handicapping conditions, poverty, and health problems that often lead to difficulties in school.[6]

"Will My Child Be Safe?"

Karen and Marina fear for their children's safety. They have known violence and drug abuse, and they worry that they will not be able to provide a safe environment.

Daphne, 18: *I really love my son, and I know the most important thing is for him to feel safe. I'll do anything it takes to keep him safe. I live with my mom now, just us and the baby, and that makes me feel safe.*

I know it's important for me to continue in school and become a child care worker so I can keep him with me when I work. That way I know nothing bad will happen to him because I'll be there to watch.

He's six months old now so Mom and I are enough for him, but I know there ought to be a good man in his life sometime. I don't know how to make that happen.

Marina, 15: *I hope the world won't end in my lifetime. I don't think it will. I think I have control over my life. I am sure going to try, and I think I can manage. You know, I keep a journal and I write the story of my life. It isn't done yet.*

I'm expecting twins, and you want to know what I worry about? I worry about living, about a place where my babies can enjoy life with no fighting, no violence, no drugs, no smoking dope. I don't know how I'll do that.

People talk to me about adoption. I know it would solve the problem, but I don't want to give them up. They're mine. I

carried them. I'm waiting for them. I was excited when I
found out I was pregnant, but I'm not now. Two is too many.
But I wouldn't give them up.

Kids Count agrees that it's a violent world. The violent death
rate of teens aged 15-19 rose 10 percent (from 63 per thousand to
69 per thousand) from 1985-1993.[7] Males comments that drug
death rates, which declined by 25 percent from 1973-1983, have
risen again, by 50 percent from 1983-1993.[8] It's dangerous out
there, and it will take all of the skills teen mothers have to
protect their children. They'll have an even harder time doing it
alone if they don't have their partners or society behind them.

Marianne and Diana, themselves victims of abuse, are
stressed about hurting their children themselves and about not
being able to protect them from harm by others.

Marianne, 16: *My baby is my world. If anything happened to*
her, I'd die. I worry all the time. I was raped three times by
people I knew, and I worry about my child being hurt sexu-
ally, mentally, and emotionally. I diaper her very carefully
and very slowly so I'll be sure not to hurt her.

I'm also worried about guys. I don't want to be molested
again. They think sex is love. I'm still drinking, but I'm very
careful. I tell my mom to not let me drink more than two
drinks. When my feet start tingling I know it's too much
alcohol. And I don't want to get drunk because I'm afraid I'll
hurt my baby.

I worry about my baby becoming an alcoholic, a druggie,
about someone hurting her, about her getting diseased, about
her falling. If she leaves this world, I will die, too. My love
overcomes me, fills me with joy, I cry happy tears. My baby is
the only one in the world who truly loves me. My mother says
she loves me, but it's not real, not like my baby's love.

I also worry about drunk drivers, auto accidents, someone

taking my baby away from me, heaven and hell, and who will care for her if I can't. I have a lot to worry about.

Diana, 17: *I'm so scared now about raising him. I know I won't hit him, but it scares me to think I might. I'll hurt my- self before I'll hurt him. My tolerance is short. I know it's because of drugs, but I have a grip on it.*

I'm scared about his father, too, that he'll try to do some- thing to hurt him and to hurt us. I'm worried about his grow- ing up. Will he listen to me? Will he stay away from drugs?

Reporting data in the state of Maine, *Maine Kids Count* warns: 18,457 cases of neglect, sexual abuse, physical abuse, or emotional abuse were reported in 1995-96, i.e. 15.2 per thou- sand, compared with the U.S. rate of 14.3 per thousand.[9] That's a lot of children to worry about.

Problem of Money

Supporting their children — that's what keeps Shunika and Joanne worrying and struggling:

Shunika, 18: *And do I worry about us? I sure do. I worry that I will not be able to provide for her financially. I'm going on to college next year, and I'm grateful for the help my parents are now willing to give me. I'll work, too, and I worry that I won't have enough time or energy to spend with her.*

I worry about how to tell her about her father, a man who does not represent the good things I want her to know and to be. I worry about the role models she'll have in her life, and how I will protect her from bad influences. I worry that she will follow my path and be a teenage single mom.

I don't put all my energy into worrying; I also plan and work hard to make the good things happen. I promise myself that this flower will be properly nurtured, no matter how much work it takes.

Joanne, 16: *I worry a lot. I worry about what kind of child she will be when she grows up. She's 15 months now, and very easy, but she'll be growing up, and what then? What kind of dangers will there be for her? Will she be good or bad? What do I do about that? I worry about money. I plan to become a nurse, and then I should be able to make a living. Now I have to finish high school, and I can do that with Mom's help. I had to give up working because getting a sitter is a real problem.*

Sex and America's Teenagers has the data. Women who have their first child as a teenager receive lower hourly wages and earn less annually than women who do not bear a child until they reach adulthood. In fact, teenage mothers earn about 50 percent of the income of those who first give birth in their twenties; a large proportion of the country's 24 million teenagers live in families that have difficulty providing such basics as food, clothing, and shelter, according to this report.[10] These teens know firsthand that it's going to be hard, but still they plan to get the education to try to do it.

And Other Worries . . .

Rosalyn, at 23 no longer a teenager, now the mother of a 7-year old son, worries about AIDS:

Rosalyn, 23: *I'm praying a lot, waiting for the news about whether I have AIDS, going to school to finish this degree, and then planning to go on to the University next year to start work on a B.S. degree.*

Should Rosalyn, sexually active since she was 15, worry? AASA's *Teenage Pregnancy* indicates she has reason to do so. "Nearly one-fourth of the individuals infected with . . . AIDS . . . are between 20 and 30 years old. Since AIDS has an average incubation period of five to seven years, most of these adults were infected as teenagers."[11]

It appears that Rosalyn and all of the other teen mothers have good reason to worry. They want to be good mothers. That's their first concern. They're willing to do what it takes, but they know the obstacles they face.

They need to be educated so they can provide for their children. But they also need to find the time to "be there" for them while they are growing up. They know from their own experiences that without someone to talk to and someone to listen, their kids won't do any better than they did. They, too, will become parents too young. Some will get into the wrong crowd and do the wrong things.

These moms know they're going to do it alone for the most part, and they know money is going to be tight. They already know how tired they're going to be because right now they're fighting for time to sleep. But they're going to try so their kids will grow up whole, with positive self-esteem. They want the world to know they really care about that.

In spite of their youth and inexperience, in spite of the loss of their own childhood, and for some, their own lack of good parenting, these young women were seriously concerned about being good mothers. "I'll love him as hard as I can," said one, expressing the feelings of so many of them.

Why Didn't They Think *First?*

"Wouldn't you think they would have thought about some of
this before they had sex? Before they got pregnant?" Adults ask
these questions, and worry about other young women doing the
same thing. I wondered if the teens could tell me.

I asked myself some questions before I asked the teens what
went on in their heads before they had sex and after they had a
baby. Was the pregnancy intentional? If it was, and there is little
research to support the issue of intentionality, then we really can
ask the question about consequences. If the pregnancy was
unintended, then we have no question. But, some teens say, "I
wanted a baby." I'd still question intentionality because we know
enough about the developmental stages of children to know that
at 13, 14, and even at 15, teens do not fully realize the
consequences of their actions.

They may think they are competent to raise a child because
they took care of younger siblings; they may think they are emotionally mature enough because they are physically able to conceive a child; or they may be counting on help from their mothers or grandmothers. But can they, with their limited experience,
really internalize the mother role? Can they see ahead to the
commitment, the frustrations, the responsibility, the sacrifices of
their own needs that are necessary to raise a child? Can their
preview of coming attractions include the mood swings that the
intense loving and unceasing demands of a new baby thrust upon
a new mother? We know that even older mothers, presumably
more experienced and more mature, sometimes have great
difficulty coping with firstborns. How can we expect an emerg-
ing woman to be prepared for the stresses of motherhood when it
is likely she is still working out her own childhood issues?

No, my guess would be that, whether planned or unplanned,
even if they do *think* about what it means to be a young mother,
they don't *know* what it means. I'd rephrase the question to ask,

"Didn't they know what being a young mother means?" This answer is clear. No, they didn't before, but they're learning. Perhaps they'd like to spare younger teens their pain and worries.

Advising Younger Teens

Even though they find out only through their own experience, hope springs eternal with me, so I asked them what they would say to younger teens if they had the chance. What would they tell them? They weren't sure it would make any difference because they knew they never listened to their parents when they were that age. "But," they said, "tell them. Just maybe they'll hear it from us."

Brenda, 16: *I want girls to know it's not all fun and games. It's hard. I go to school, spend an hour or so with my baby, do the laundry, go to work, get home and sterilize bottles, make formula. I'm behind in my school work, but I need to work to have money for my child so I can't really help it. But I also need to graduate high school in order to get better work, so I have to figure it out. I want to go on to college and learn*

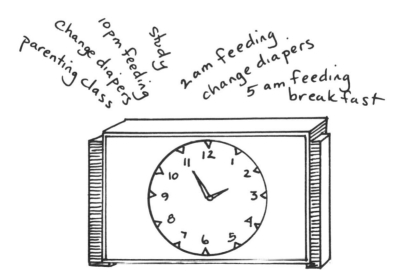

more so I can get a better job and do even more for him.

Mom won't babysit for me just to go out and play, but she will to let me go to work and to school. My social life is gone. I have no time to go out or to see friends, but that's the way it is when you have a baby and you have to work.

Helena, 17: *I'm just bursting to say some things to younger girls, girls from 12 years old and up.*

Listen to me. You might think a guy is perfect, but one night isn't worth changing your whole life for. You might think you can handle it because you've taken care of a brother or a cousin. But this isn't part-time. You have to be strong. If you still want to party, you're not ready for a baby. If you don't have the money to take care of a baby, you're not ready. If you like to come home from school and just relax and not have other jobs to do, you're not ready. If you can't buy your baby what he needs, if you like to sleep a lot, if you like to not worry a lot, you're not ready.

There's a long, hard road in front of us, and I'm beginning to see it more clearly. I know I can do it for us and I know I will, but I'm not going to sit here and tell you it's easy. I'm telling you it's tough, and keep that in mind when some sweet-talking guy shows up and tells you he loves you. If you're not ready to be a mother, forget it.

Jacqueline, 16: *I think about the girls who are thirteen out there and hope they'll read my story and be influenced by it. I want to tell them not to have sex before they get married. I thought it couldn't happen to me, but I ran out of birth control pills and it did. It turned my life around, and that's gotta be a good thing, but like my mom said, it's too bad I had to get pregnant to do that.*

Jenine, 16: *I'd like to give some advice to younger girls. I'd like to tell them a lot of things, to lecture to them, but most kids* *that age don't want to listen. If I could show them how hard it is to be this age and be pregnant, about to become a mother, maybe they'd listen. I didn't care at 12 what people said, but if I really saw something, it made an impact.*

Mindy, 16: *I'm glad you're writing a book about being a teenage mother because the stuff they have out there doesn't talk about what it's really like. They tell you how to take care of the baby and all that, but they don't tell you how hard it is, or how lonely, or how you wish it didn't happen. I want to tell you about that. And I want to put this in your book so maybe younger kids will listen, though I know I never listened.*

I could be living my life as a teenager, going to school with my own class, graduating high school with them, and being a kid. I knew I could get pregnant if I wasn't careful, and I knew I could get AIDS, too, but I was sure it would never happen to me. So I went ahead and had sex, and now I'm a mother at 16, just like my mom was.

Shawn, 16: *I know there are kids out there, younger than me, who maybe won't want to hear this, but I'd like to tell them anyhow: don't have a baby before you can afford it; get through school. It's too hard to do all this, get up at night with the baby, then go to school in the morning. But if you do get pregnant and have a baby, don't drop out like I did when I had her. I did come back, though, and I am going to finish.*

Do They Understand What Parenting Means?

"Do they understand what it means to have a baby?" adults ask. They didn't, but they do now. Now most are without a partner, with a baby, and with barely enough money to make ends meet. They know how tired and how stressed they are. They know that their only chance to become independent is to finish high school, to train for a career, to get a job. They know how hard it is to juggle child care with these responsibilities. They wonder why they didn't listen to people who tried to tell them how it was, and they admit that it would have been better to wait before they had a child. They told their stories to younger teens with the hope they might listen.

Every parent who reads this chapter will say, "Advice to young teens? What's the point? They never listen to us." They are quite right. The teen mothers told me that some of their mothers, many of whom had been teen parents themselves, tried to tell them not to have babies too young, and that they never listened. But, these teens told me, they might have listened to other teens, especially if they were talking from their own experience and were not preaching.

They hope their advice will get to younger girls, that they will listen and be spared the overwhelming problems of being a young mother. Most of all, they hope these young people will have the opportunity to be kids themselves before they become mothers.

A group in the South tripped over each other as they asked me to tell young teens: "Come spend a week with me and my baby. Get up early and feed her and dress her. Get her ready to take the bus to school with you. Get yourself ready for school, too, and then make the bus on time. Then go to school and stay awake. Come home, take care of the baby, do the laundry, do the cooking, do your homework, give her a bath, clean up after supper, fold the laundry, take a shower, go to bed so you can get up early in the morning. Unless she wakes you during the night. If you're not ready for this, don't get pregnant."

Teen Moms' List of Don'ts

As much as they hated the *don'ts* themselves, here's the list of *don'ts* they came up with:

- Don't have sex too early.
- Don't have sex if . . .
  — you're not ready to get pregnant.
  — you don't want to get AIDS.
  — you're not willing to use protection.
- Don't sleep with anybody unless you're ready for the responsibility of being a parent. Once you're stuck, you're stuck.
- Don't believe the guys when they say they'll love you forever because they lose interest the minute you get pregnant and you get fat.
- If you don't have the money, forget it!
- Don't drop out of school, not ever. Not before you get pregnant, and not after.
- Don't get pregnant if . . .
  — you're not ready to be a full-time mother.
  — you're not ready to give up being a kid yourself.
  — you want to complete your education without being hassled.
  — you don't want to be tired all the time.
  — you don't have the money.
  — you're not old enough to be independent of your parents.
- And . . . if you do get pregnant, and you thought you were woman enough to sleep with a guy,
  — then be woman enough to do whatever it takes to be a good mother.

We can't just brush aside this issue and say, "Sure, they have good reason to worry. But why did they get themselves into this mess in the first place?" We have to acknowledge that their worries are our worries. We have to hope that young teens can be reached by teen parents who know how hard it is. Their children born and yet unborn are the children of our future.

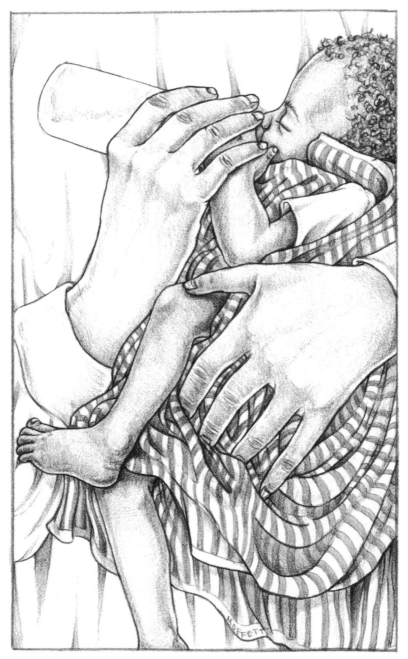

6

Feelings about Welfare and Independence

"They have babies just for the welfare," they say.

The public concern over welfare peaked in September of 1996 at which time the Congress sent the President a welfare reform bill. He signed it reluctantly. It "ended welfare as we know it," a campaign promise he had made in the 1992 election year. The sponsors of the bill hoped to change what they considered an entitlement mentality by limiting lifetime benefits to five years; by enforcing the qualification that the head of the family must work within two years or lose benefits; by legislating that an unmarried teen parent could receive benefits only if she were under 18, stayed in school, and lived with an adult.

The weeks and months preceding President Clinton's signing of the new welfare law in the fall of 1996 were frenzied with activity. Lawmakers harangued, public meetings bristled, and the media bubbled. Radio, TV, and the written press over-flowed with commentary. Liberals battled conservatives; radicals battered moderates; neighbors hassled neighbors. Everyone who paid taxes had an opinion.

"End Welfare as We Know It"

It started out slowly. It was 1992 and the Republican Con-gress was hard at work on the budget for their Contract with America. The President, having promised to "end welfare as we know it" in 1992, was in a political bind. "If Congress will send me a welfare reform bill that is tough on work instead of tough on children and weak on work, I will proudly sign it," he said.[1]

By May of '96 he announced his own plan. Teen mothers, to collect a welfare check, had to stay in school, live at home, attend parenting classes, and establish paternity in order to obtain child support. House Republicans attacked his plan, saying that it not only kept welfare in federal hands but also sustained it as a way of life. The battle speeded up. Everyone wanted credit for reform, well aware that the American public was flooding the airwaves with their concerns about how their tax money was being used. Talk shows were drumming up rage, and the Con-gress and the President were playing to the galleries.

By July of 1996, a welfare reform bill had passed the House and was poised to be passed in the Senate. The lawmakers were preparing for the August political conventions at which they wanted to take credit for the reform.

Thoughtful social commentators like Constance Buchanan, the Associate Dean of Harvard's Divinity School, bemoaned the fact that none of this concern and activity addressed the real source of the problem — poverty. How could poor women, she asked, unable to afford child care, be expected to work and take care of their children, to keep the social fabric of the family from unraveling, and to do all this without the concerted assistance of mainstream institutions?[2] But hers was not the voice of the multitudes.

At the opposite end of the political spectrum, commentators like Jeff Jacoby were decrying the liberals and castigating both the states and the federal government for not being tough enough. Jacoby blamed welfare for all the ills of society. He complained that welfare had lured millions of girls and women into ruining their lives by bribing them to have children before they had husbands. It detached fathers from families, he said, teaching them to be predators rather than providers. It biased whole neighborhoods against work and spread the delusion that the poor need not help themselves.[3]

Many states, wanting to be ready for the time when the federal government would turn welfare money over to them, had already received federal waivers for reform. They had spent months in preparation. Both liberals and conservatives experimented with limiting payments to mothers who conceived additional children while on welfare and to women who wouldn't identify the father. They also were working toward establishing a lifetime limit on benefits.

Steve Goldsmith, the mayor of Indianapolis, saw real possibilities in reform, saying America's cities could reap the benefits of welfare in four ways. He said states could encourage responsible fatherhood, provide jobs, reform the bureaucracy, and use the flexibility only a city can provide, as opposed to the larger, more cumbersome federal bureaucracy.[4]

On August 22, 1996, the Senate passed the welfare reform law, Public Law 104-93, HR 3734, and the President signed it. His reasoning may have been political — he would be able to say he supported welfare reform at the Democratic convention where he would be nominated for his second term. Or it may have been pragmatic — he knew he couldn't do better.

The conventions over and the President nominated, the bill took effect on October 1. Now the states would have block grants, would make their own decisions regarding the use of the money, but would still have federal guidelines they must follow.

It didn't take long for the problems to surface. By the first of the year, the President, realizing that the shortage of jobs and the insistence that welfare recipients work in order to collect checks were in conflict with each other, began calling on industry to provide such jobs.[5] Commentators were busy again, comparing reductions from the federal benefits, and disparities between the states. They now ranged from $923 to $120 per month for a family of three, depending on the state's economy and/or philosophy.[6]

States wrestled with their new problems. In addition to creating and finding jobs, they were working on providing incentives for industry, getting more involved with child care, redeploying social services, relocating workers, and driving their computers into implementing the new law.

How would the states continue to address the distribution of money to single teen mothers? Would the statistics on single mother (especially teen) births go down? Would fewer people require welfare assistance? Would those on welfare be able to move off the rolls sooner? It's hard to predict how the new law will affect teen mothers and teen pregnancy in the future, but surely people of every political and social persuasion will be watching.

The interviews that follow were conducted before the new law went into effect, but the problems they address have not changed.

Pat Hartstein, the director of an alternative middle and high school in St. Petersburg, Florida, commented, "The majority of the girls here don't want welfare. They want more for their lives, but they lack the confidence that they can make it on their own. We're teaching them that education is the only way out of whatever kind of ghetto they're in, black or white. I know about welfare. I grew up on it. What a stigma that leaves on kids. You're on welfare, people say, and you lower your head.

"Sometimes, when I was little, we moved into the house at midnight, just like we moved out of the old one, because we couldn't pay the rent. My father was sent to jail, and he spent most of my growing-up years there. Mom cared for us alone the best she could.

"We lived mostly in housing projects, and even as a little girl, I sensed the discrimination. Once a month, when the check arrived, we'd eat good. Mom would buy bologna and special rolls, and she made us hoagies. We ate well for a couple of weeks until the money started to run out. Then we'd eat creatively. That meant cubed potatoes with ground beef a few nights a week. You could buy ground beef then for three pounds for a dollar, and that stretched the money for us.

"My father was in jail for writing bad checks, but he'd get home now and then. We four kids were aged 2 to 13 when my mother died. Father died of cancer at 55, and Mother died of pleurisy and a broken heart and body at 43. She'd struggled all those years on welfare with no support from my father. The worst part for her was the stigma of being on welfare and having no respect from the neighbors.

"After my mother died, I was raised by my grandmother in a middle-class suburb. She had to rely on welfare to take care of us kids, though, and the welfare stigma continued."[7]

"I'd Rather Work"

When I talked with the teen mothers about welfare, most said they hated it. They especially resented the fact that people

thought they had babies just to collect it. They were distressed at
being called welfare queens, and they were hurt by people
looking down on them. They said welfare made them feel
inferior. Over and over they told me they'd much rather work,
but they were too young. If they were old enough, they had a
very hard time going to school, taking care of their child, and
working.

They want to finish high school so they can make their own
living and not be dependent on welfare. Like Pat Hartstein, they
prefer independence to welfare, and they talk bravely about plans
to support themselves and their children. They also talk about the
problems they have seeing these plans through. The more
determined ones are sure they will overcome the obstacles.

Candy, 18: *He's 18, too, and he's a good guy. I'm still with him;
we live together in our own home. Have for a year. He works,
went to school and graduated with honors, and I have a part-
time job. I go to this high school for teen moms and it's great.
I get Medicaid for my daughter for a year but I don't get food
stamps. We're not on welfare, and we never have been. We've
always managed to be independent.*

*I'm going to make life better for her than it was for me. I
never had enough money to have brand name clothes and*

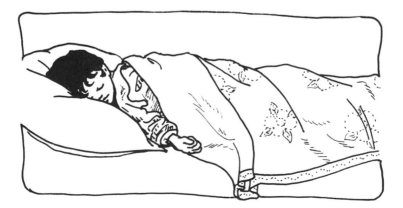

shoes. She'll have them.

My mom never thought I'd make anything of myself, but my sister would. I'll prove to her that I can do it. I'll graduate high school, and I'll go on to become a mental health therapist. I'll go to college, and I'll graduate. I can do it. They say I can't, but I can and I will.

Fran, 18: *With the money the baby's father sometimes gives me and AFDC, I just get by, but it's not enough and I hate getting it. I'm job hunting now, but so far I haven't found anything. I'll take anything because I resent people thinking I'm lazy, and I don't feel comfortable taking handouts.*

I plan to finish high school, then get my LPN. I'll do it, whatever it takes. I want my child to grow up to be independent, to respect himself and other people, and to get a good education. It's okay for him to be raised by a single mom as long as I can give him a good life.

Lila, 15: *My own life is hard. I want to try my best to finish high school. I'm smart and I want to go to college. I want to study medicine and become a doctor. One day I think the baby's dad and I will get married, and he wants to go to college, too. It's going to be hard, but one day we may be able to get married and be a family just like normal people.*

Paula, 16: *I did without welfare when I didn't have a baby, and I'll do without it now. I'm 16 and my baby is four months old. I work at a restaurant fourteen hours a week, and I'm going to graduate high school.*

The dad is 20, and he's a good father. He comes home after work to help with the baby, and we all get along fine. We live here with his mom.

I plan to go to community college to take up child care. I'd be good at it, I know.

Joyce, 17: *I don't feel good about being on welfare. It doesn't make me feel good about myself. My family says get the welfare while you can, but I don't like it. When I work for something for myself and I buy something, I cherish it more because I did it.*

I'm going to work for everything for him and for me, and I know it will make me a stronger person. When I was a little girl everything was given to me and I didn't appreciate it, but now I'll work for what we need and for what I want, and I'll appreciate it.

Tanya, 18: *We were on welfare for a year when we first moved here from Arizona. We hated it, and Mom became a nurse so she could make good money to raise us. We had a good home with no drugs and no alcohol. She was a good mom. She provided for us, she loved us, and gave us a lot of support. She showed affection and attention, too. So it comes naturally to me to be a good mom, even though it's hard with my three kids so close in age.*

I'm doing okay, staying in school, and trying to finish high

*school. Mom helps me at home as much as she can, but it's
hard to get all of them ready to take the bus with me to
school. They get great care here in the nursery, and I
appreciate this school a lot.*

*I get $345 a month from AFDC, but no child support from
the fathers. It's not enough to get by, but my dad helps and my
mom does, too. So I plan to finish here and go on to VoTech
to get my associate degree. I'm going to college to get a
nursing degree. It's the only way for my kids and me to have a
life. I'll find a way. I will.*

Ruby, 16: *I'm moving to the state where my baby's dad is so we
can be together. I plan to finish high school, go to college,
and then go to law school. I'm a good student and a good
reader. I plan to get a part-time job while I'm finishing high
school and get a babysitter there.*

*I'll find a way. I'll get scholarships. I'm not afraid, and I
know I can do it. The dad is a good guy. He doesn't do drugs
or alcohol. He'll be there for us.*

*I'll miss this school because they're so good with the baby
and it's right for me. I get to see him during breaks, and he
gets to come with me every day. I don't know what I'll find in
my new place, but I'm sure it will be all right and we're going
to make it.*

But, as Pat Hartstein told us, many teens lack the confidence
to overcome the internal and external obstacles they know they
face. Money is high on their worry list. Their own histories of
poor progress in school, and the drugs and violence they experienced at home and in the neighborhood may get in their way.

Adrienne, 17: *We'll live with my mom and I will finish high
school. I talk well, and I think I'd be good at telemarketing.
Mom says if I go on to more school after high school, she will
babysit for me.*

I still worry about things. I worry about being a better student, and I worry about being a better reader. I don't read well, and I can't seem to learn.

Joanne, 16: *I worry about money, too. I plan to become a pediatric nurse, and then I should be able to make a living. I have to finish high school, and I can do that with Mom's help, but I had to give up working now because getting a sitter is a real problem.*

Rhonda, 17: *After I finish high school I want to go to a vocational school to take a medical secretary's course. I can be a good student when I want to be, but lately I've been so stressed out about money and about her father that I haven't been doing well in school.*

Tammy, 14: *Being a mom isn't hard. I'm happy to have my baby but I wouldn't do it again. I don't want any more kids till I can afford it. I want to be a homicide detective.*

I saw my mom get shot. I think it was drug related. She says no, but I think so. She was hurt, but she's okay. She has only one kidney now, and her liver and bladder aren't good, but she's the healthiest she's ever been.

A group of teens I spoke with in a southern town told me they would like to work, but there just weren't any jobs for them. Others, mothers at 15, said they couldn't work because they weren't old enough. Welfare wasn't enough to get by on, and the men who impregnated them wouldn't accept responsibility for being the fathers. Sometimes they said they were sterile; it couldn't be theirs. If they did agree to paternity, they couldn't be found, and the young mothers couldn't collect child support.

Considering Society's Role

What problems do these issues raise for society? We know about poverty, and we know about the absence of jobs for poorly educated young women. "The law merely requires the states to cut welfare caseloads and limit the duration of public assistance," says Kuttner in the *Boston Globe.* "If jobs are not available, people will simply join the growing legions of beggars."[8]

The teens told us, and the data confirmed, that contrary to the popular belief that they have babies just to collect welfare, most do not like welfare, nor do they have their babies to collect welfare. According to Luker, it stands to reason that if welfare encouraged early childbearing, then places which had more generous benefits should show an increase in the number of unmarried teenage mothers. But the United States provides less support for single mothers than any other industrialized country, yet has one of the highest proportions of teenage mothers.[9]

A comparison of Mississippi and Minnesota illustrates the point. Mississippi ranks lowest with its monthly welfare grant for a family of three ($120) and highest in its birthrate to 15-17-year old women (20 percent above the state median); Minnesota ranks among the highest monthly grants ($532) and lowest in the birthrate to 15-17-year-olds (20 percent below the state median).[10]

The young mothers are doing whatever they can to become independent, but they find it very hard. The majority of fathers are not there to help with the child or to pay child support; the teen mothers are trying to finish high school, are too young to get jobs, and they don't have enough time for taking care of their babies and finishing school. Most of them live at home with their own mothers, and they want to get away from that dependency as well, a prime motivator for finishing high school and being able to get a good job.[11]

And what does research indicate? The stereotype held by many, that people on welfare love the free ride and are mostly African Americans from the inner city ghetto, is contradicted by

the statistics that report that most welfare recipients are white,
live in the suburbs or rural areas, and are off welfare within
twelve months.[12]

Fifty percent of recipients can't work because they are too
young or too old. One-third of all children living in poverty are
children of families who work, but who are still below the
poverty level. The studies term this group the "Working Poor."[13]
Other studies show that 80 percent of American pregnancies are
unplanned or unintended, again contradicting the belief that
young women have babies for welfare money.[14]

Study after study corroborates the fact that the major deter-
mining factor is poverty with the accompanying problems of
crime, drugs, hopelessness, lack of responsible male role models,
unsupervised homes, and lack of self-esteem, all of which either
expose young women to sexual abuse or predispose them to be
easy prey to men who promise them the love and security they
are looking for.

What Happens Now?

What's going to happen now? Will the new federal and state
statutes solve the problems many feel were created by the old
ones? Will the new laws exacerbate the problems the old laws
were trying to solve?

We don't know the answers yet, but we do know that the
states are deeply engaged, often passionately, in the implementa-
tion of the federal and state statutes and policies, and that the
welfare analysts are looking hard at the variables.

Since each state, given a block grant by the federal government, has wide latitude within the federal guidelines, there are
many variables among them. Some of the variables analysts are
looking at are: the range of benefits; the periods of time before
welfare checks terminate; the cut-off time after a recipient finds
work; ranges in the limit on lifetime benefits; the variety in

deductions taken before the benefit is determined.

Another important variable is the amount of time states have been working on their plans. Some, such as Wisconsin, Massachusetts, and Michigan, have been working on changing welfare for a number of years; other states are plunging in with untried plans. Regardless of whether a state has strong liberal traditions such as Hawaii and Minnesota, or has a reputation for being conservative, i.e., Texas and South Carolina, they are united in their drive to shift recipients into the workforce. They reason that the economy is active now. Who knows what will happen later?[15]

What's the rush and why the panic? Why the passionate reactions of both conservatives and liberals? The rush and the panic can be explained in pragmatic terms. According to the new law, states will be required to spend at least 80 percent of their own funds, reducing the block grant given them by the federal government by five percent, if they fail to meet the work participation rate for welfare recipients. If they do meet the job requirements, they will need to spend 75 percent of their own funds. This five percent leeway looms as a real saving for states, many of which are hard pressed to fulfill their welfare obligations with their own money.[16]

With so many people to place in jobs and so few jobs to be filled, states feel stressed. The law requires that adult recipients go to work within two years of receiving aid, and that doesn't give them much time. The penalty for not meeting the requirement adds to their burden. Each succeeding year after failure to meet the deadline, the state's grant will be reduced by two percent, topping off at a maximum deduction of 21 percent. That's a pretty powerful motivator![17]

Why the passionate reactions to the change? This question is not answered with "bottom line" statistics. This question digs up emotions based on philosophical, psychological, economic,

sociological, religious, and educational beliefs — values people hold close to their hearts. We're talking about emotions here, not rational thinking.

How will this affect the poor? What about the children? How can a country this rich treat its poorest so badly? These questions are countered by others. What about personal responsibility? What's the matter with work? What happened to the values of our founding fathers? The moderates try to look both left and right. How can we solve this problem, they ask. What is the best way to protect those living in poverty, yet address the realities of the budget and the deficit and not promote dependence on public assistance?

We all have questions that need answering, questions we ask while we are waiting and watching. Will the states be able to meet the federal requirements for job placement? Will the states be able to bring the out-of-wedlock birthrates down? Will teen mothers be able to manage better when living with their families? Or will they suffer more abuse?

Will child care be available, if necessary, so teens can work, finish high school, or go on to higher education? What about health care? What will happen to the indigent after the five-year lifetime benefit limit is imposed? What will happen to the states if they can't meet the requirements and, as a consequence, receive less federal funding?

Well, we could say, it's their responsibility now. The states are establishing the rules, and the teens and their families have to measure up. But President Clinton sees it differently. Speaking of the new law, he commented that now that it is enacted, everyone who has ever said a disparaging word about the old welfare system should begin to take responsibility for making the new one work.[18] I agree.

We don't have the old entitlement program to kick around any more. A new one is being born, state by state. It's not just in the hands of the federal government; it's not just in the hands of the states; it's not just in the hands of the teens and their families. Now it's in the hands of all of us. It's everyone's baby.

7

Changed Lives —
The Pain
and the Promise

Throughout the interview process I struggled to find a way
to address these young females who were either pregnant or
mothers. Their ages ranged from 13 to 18. Some looked like
children, some had children's bodies and grown-up faces, some
had grown-up bodies and children's faces, and some looked like
grown women. "Girls" just didn't sound right when talking with
pregnant or parenting teens. "Kids" was a real no-no; the first
time I said it, two or three of them bristled. "Ladies" has a
connotation this generation of young people doesn't relate to,
and "Women" sounds peculiar.

So most of the time I used their first names, even when
talking with a group, and addressed the group with words of
welcome and thanks for their willingness to participate in my
research for the book. In the North "I want to welcome you . . . "

worked very well, and in the South I sometimes lapsed into "I want to welcome y'all . . . ," but most of the time it was "I want to welcome each of you . . . " and that seemed to work the best. The one thing these young women were looking for above all else was to be treated with dignity and respect.

This aspect of my questioning was one of the most poignant for me as a teacher, parent, grandparent, and in my very long-term memory, a picture of myself as a teen. In those years people didn't really talk about teenagers — we were high schoolers, or junior high schoolers, but still we were 13 or 14 or 15, and we weren't grown-ups yet.

My afternoons were spent at my friend Ellie's house where the musical group gathered because Ellie sang, her sister played the piano, and her mother was a wonderfully warm woman who loved the group, the music, and the noise. We ate our way through boxes of Fannie Farmer candy and homemade ice cream sodas and frappes, scooping the ice cream from the freezer ice cube trays because that was the only place to keep ice cream in the "old days." While we ate, the trumpeter played Glenn Miller music with Margie's piano and our voices as accompaniment.

I'd think about those days, our freedom from worry about anything except school and boys, even though money was tight and many of us had part-time jobs on the weekend. How were these girls-kids-young women managing, their childhoods already behind them? I thought many of them were heroic, patiently getting ready to take care of a child or, already mothers, caring for a child while trying to finish high school, and some-times working as well.

"How Has Your Life Changed?"

I asked a group in the South to tell me how their lives had changed. They said: "I have to be responsible now. I have to care about what I do. I can't hang out with stoners. They're childish and I have to be grown up."

"I have to take care of my baby or CPS (Children's Protective Services) will take him away," they said.

Ellie and I had worried about dates — these teens were worried about losing their babies!

In private interviews, several new mothers told me nothing had really changed for them. They had nothing before, so they felt they had nothing to give up:

Rosamund, 15: *Being a mother didn't really change my life. I never did anything before. I didn't have a lot of friends, so it's not too different now except that wherever I go, she goes, too.*

But some were mourning their lost childhood:

Alana, 15: *I'll never be a kid again, and I'm only 15.*

Joanne, 16: *I know my life has changed a lot. I can't party . because I have no sitter and very little money to spend. But most of all I'm too tired. I have to get up at 3 a.m. to feed her, and some nights she's up most of the night. I hope when she gets older it will get better.*

Tracy, 16: *Before I got pregnant I had a lot of friends. I hung out and partied. I was a normal teen. A lot of statistics say kids like me who get pregnant so young and not married come from poor backgrounds. But I've never been without even though my mom raised us alone. She had her first kid at 18 and got married, but they were divorced after three kids. She worked so hard to take care of us. She went to school and became an RN. She got us a house, a car, and she loved us. She's my heroine.*

One was mourning her lost figure and her modeling career:

Tameka, 18: *I modeled before I got pregnant and I loved it, but being pregnant changed my life.*

Some See Positive Change

Others could see only positive change. I had been prepared for hearing that things were awful. It was no surprise to me that some said they were missing being a teen, that they had to give up too much. But I was completely shaken the first time I heard a young mother say things had changed for the better. Being pregnant and having a baby had turned their lives around.

When I began to probe about what that meant, they talked about what their lives were like before they got pregnant, and then it began to make sense to me that this life was better. They told me that being a mother, being in this alternative school, or living in this group home was good for them because they had escaped their abusive families, the gangs, the crime, the violence, and the drugs that had been part of their lives before.

"How did it go over in the neighborhood when everyone found out you were pregnant at 13 (or 14 or 15)?"

"It was okay," they said.

Backing this perception is the reality that in some neighborhoods having a child while one is a teenager is not considered particularly deviant behavior. In fact, for many it is a rite of passage.[1]

Ginger, 13: *You know, I would still be part of a gang if this didn't happen. All my friends are in them. I used to always fight. Getting pregnant saved me from the gang, and from an abusive home. Our gang was tight, but I'm not going near them anymore.*

Jacqueline, 16: *I was arrested for shoplifting before I got pregnant, but I gave that up, too. I gave up drugs. I used to do marijuana every day and cocaine on weekends. My boyfriend supplied the drugs because he had them to sell.*

I was a dropout then, and I was a patient at the hospital for trying suicide. I overdosed on Tylenol and planned to slit my wrists, but they got me to the hospital before I did that. They said I had severe depression. They got me a psychiatrist and put me on medication for eight months. Before that I used to leave home and not come back for weeks at a time. I stayed anywhere I could.

Getting pregnant turned my life around. Now I'm in school again. I have a different point of view now. Is it mother instinct? I don't know. It's so real, and I feel like I can accomplish something now. I plan to finish high school, and I plan to raise this baby.

Rhonda, 17: *My life really changed when I had my baby. I look at my friends now and they're into drugs and partying, but I'm not there now. I could be harming myself and then my baby, so I don't go with them.*

Before I got pregnant I was into acid, pot and alcohol. Now I don't touch anything except maybe a wine cooler once in a while. I know I could be having fun in high school now, cheerleading. I even had a part-time job and money to spend, but this is the way I chose to go, so I have to make it work.

With unusual insight, some recognized that they had become less self-centered, and had changed habits they now thought were bad.

Dena, 18: *Until I got pregnant I didn't care at all, but once I knew I was going to be a mother, I began to study, to take care of myself, to eat right, and to work hard. It worked for me because now I'm doing well with Tommy, school, and work.*

Joyce, 17: *I spend everything I have on him. If I see a really nice outfit for me, and I love clothes, I have to let it be and buy diapers and food. I was into clothes, and hairdos, and jewelry, but now he comes first. He's almost two. It's not about me anymore, now it's about him.*

Jewel, 17: *I can't blame my mom for what I did, and I can't blame alcohol or drugs, either. I come from a long line of alcoholics on both sides of the family, and I was sure I wasn't going to do that. It was none of those things. It was just me. I wasn't happy at school or at home, so I dropped out of both to start my own life.*

It wasn't any good with my boyfriend, either. We started fighting, and he got nasty. He didn't hit me, but he said awful things and I felt just as bad as I did in school.

I don't know what I would have done if I hadn't got pregnant, but I did, and that turned my life around. Becoming a mother changed me in other ways, too. I used to be a mess all the time, but now I keep everything clean and neat. I'm more responsible. I don't go out a lot. I stay home when I get through school, and I study and take care of my baby. I date very little, and when I do I make sure the man is clean. He has to have a piece of paper that says he is not HIV positive before I'll start going with him. I need to be alive in order to take care of my child.

Marianne, 16: *Having a baby changed my life. Before I was a mother I was bad. I was selfish; it was my way or no way. I did drugs, I did alcohol. I'm an alcoholic and I'm still work-ing that out. I went to AA and it was good, but I don't go now. I need to, but I need a sponsor and I need a ride.*

Some older teens realized that they had found a new focus in their lives when they were placed in alternative schools with relevant curriculum and caring adults. For the first time, they felt that education mattered.

Anne, 21: *There were two women who gave my life new mean-ing when I was pregnant and finishing high school. They listened, they helped me think about myself and my goals, and they helped me choose a career.*

Candy, 18: *I know I'm young to be a mother; it's a big responsibility, and I have bad days sometimes. But my boyfriend helps me, and there's a teacher here who's wonderful to me. Mom helps with the baby, and she loves her, too. I love my baby to death. I don't know what I'd be like without her.*

If my daughter has a child at 15 or 16, I'll be there for her. I'd encourage her to wait and finish high school first, but if she doesn't, I'll help her.

Sometimes I think I should have waited, but then I think it was good I didn't because this high school program is so good for me. They made me welcome, they supported me through all the emotional stuff, they make school worthwhile. I get up in the morning feeling good about going to school. I never did before.

You have to say that having a baby young is not all bad. It changed my life around.

Shanika, 18: *Something happened to me when I got pregnant, something that surprised me. It was a feeling even stronger than my negative image of myself and the negative reinforcements of my parents. Here was a baby going to be born! Here*

was a reality check! I was going to have to be a mom myself.

I had done a good job with my brother, so I had that strength to lean on, and I knew that the teenage stuff I was doing just didn't fit for me any more. My grades went from C's and D's to A's and B's, and my lifestyle changed completely. I was lucky enough to become part of a program for teenage mothers in which I had day care, alternative high school education, parenting training, and two marvelous women who went to work on my self-esteem with a vengeance. They succeeded in doing a lot with it, and I don't know how to thank them adequately for all their work and care.

Except for the two teens who felt it didn't matter because they had nothing to lose anyway, these young women knew that pregnancy and motherhood had changed their lives dramatically. They couldn't be kids themselves anymore; now they had to be mothers. To them this meant responsibility, not only to take care of a new life, but to be able to provide for that life in the future. This meant they'd better finish high school, and for some it meant they'd better go on for further education so they could get a good job.

Though most dwelt on the hard part — the growing up, the giving up — for others it was a relief to be done with the past. They got out of an abusive home, out of a life of crime, or a gang. They felt that sex wasn't going to be a big part of their lives either, for a while at least. They had lost their interest in it.

I had expected the negatives — the hard parts, the loss of their own childhoods, the financial problems and responsibilities. But their sense of being rescued from abusers and from themselves was a total surprise for me. They blessed their pregnancy for this.

The lucky girls who got into alternative high school programs that promoted their education and achievement as well as the wellbeing of their babies called it a new beginning. Others, in group homes where they felt safe for the first time, said they were rescued. I was particularly touched by the fact that they were grateful to have positive role models in their teachers and counselors. For them, this seemed to be the crucial missing piece.

Can Teen Pregnancy Be an Improvement?

I spoke with the professionals about these young women's perception that motherhood for them was a positive thing, and I asked, "Can we really believe that teen pregnancy is a good thing for these girls?"

They nodded. "Yes, we were surprised, too, by how many of these young women said this was the best thing that had ever happened to them." Even though they recognized the difficulties and losses, they appreciated the opportunities they had never had before.

They like the schools which meet their needs; they are relieved and feel safe; they like the people who are caring and responsive; and they are enjoying learning how to be good mothers. We can only imagine how hard their lives must have been before if this life is so good for them.

Even if I hadn't asked the specific question about how their lives had changed, I would have heard it in their conversations with each other. Whenever I had talked with teens during my years of teaching, their interactions were peppered with talk of boys, hairdos, nails, jeans, and parties. They don't come much more self-centered than teens in groups.

But here, whether in the North or South, the conversations had only to do with their pregnancies or their parenting. Their babies were in their minds first and last. These conversations were about health care, diapers, being good mothers, absent fathers, and the need to finish school so they could take proper care of their babies.

They had left their childhoods and teen talk behind them and were moving into adult womanhood at a frantic pace. What a struggle for them. What a challenge for us.

What does all this mean? Is this good or bad? Isn't it a good thing that a pregnant teen changes her old life? A baby pushes her into giving up drugs, shoplifting, casual sex, and being part of a gang. Isn't it good that she finds an alternative school where she restructures her life, replaces old values with new ones, and through good education finds her way to a future? Sounds good to me.

What about us? Isn't it good that we changed some of our thinking and provided the schools and nurseries and the group homes? It is unthinkable for young women, hardly more than children themselves, to be mothers. The babies have to be taken care of. So babies motivated us to intervene on the teen parents' behalf, just as they motivated the teens to change the direction of their lives. Sounds good, too.

Are we going to say, then, that having babies is good for at-risk teens? Not at all. What's wrong with this rosy picture is that all of the change — the teens and ours — should be taking place long *before* pregnancy and motherhood, not after. It's not ideal for teens to be mothers when they are not mature enough to make good decisions for themselves, let alone for another life. Our intervention is crucial to prevent too-early childbearing.

But what motivation can we provide for teens and for ourselves that is as dramatic as a helpless newborn? We have to look at their needs. What is going on in the world of these girls/ women that they find a sense of purpose and fulfillment in being mothers at so young an age? What is missing in their childhoods to make the future look so grim? What is there that could motivate them to care about changing their lifestyles in the same way that having a baby does? We heard the clues — life now had purpose, it was a reality check, they felt love, they had responsibility. What motivation can we find for ourselves that is as dramatic as a helpless newborn? What could motivate us to make the effort to provide the intervention that will prevent these young women from becoming mothers too early?

What Works?

We've looked at their stories; now let's look at the data. The research tells us that poor literacy skills are a good predictor of early childbearing. Children who don't read well are at risk for early pregnancy. We also know that poor progress in school and the ensuing loss of self-esteem is a predictor of early pregnancy. Young women who are enrolled in college preparatory curriculum in high school are far less likely to give birth than are their peers who are not planning further education. And we also know that programs that encourage teens to stay in school work, but admonishing teens to postpone childbearing doesn't.[2]

It sounds like we need to do two things. We need to provide the kind of education that fires the imagination of preteens whom we know to be at risk of early pregnancy, and we need to be the kind of warm and caring mentors that fire those imaginations.

Let me tell you about the excellent schools, homes, and nurseries where I conducted my interviews. In the best of these facilities there was an air of calm and excitement that only good schools offer. The students and their babies were safe, and more important, they felt safe. They were respected. They were accepted.

But they were not given a free ride. They were being challenged to do better than they had done as students in their old schools or as high school dropouts. They were being encouraged to finish high school, to choose higher education and/or careers in order to become self-sustaining and independent. They were

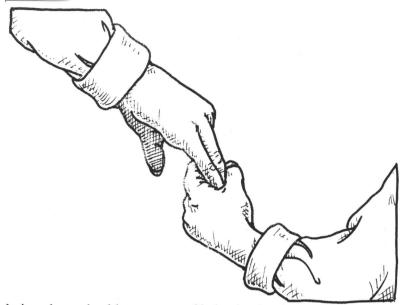

being shown healthy patterns of behavior for themselves and their children; they were being imbued with the values of hard work and achievement. In addition to the courses needed for a high school diploma, they were also taking life skills — health and sex education, successful parenting, development of positive relationships, and workforce preparation.

In all cases, the single factor that seemed to me to be the most important for these young women was the presence of positive role models, both female and male, who expressed caring and interest in them. Hope Edelman (*Motherless Daughters*) corroborates this. "The single most important factor that helps children who grow up under adverse family or social conditions to become emotionally adjusted, competent adults is the active involvement of at least one stable adult who cares," she reports.[3]

If relevant schooling and the appropriate level of caring and nurturing can turn things around for teen mothers, what might we do for teens *before* they become pregnant? We have to acknowledge that for some, motherhood seems to be the only route to feeling valued. As mothers, they feel needed and loved.

Young people's bonding with gangs is another manifestation of this need to be part of something, to be wanted. If we could give them the same sense of purpose and the same feeling of nurture they get from being mothers and, for some, gang members, quite likely we could bring about change.

If we made it our business to see that all students are able to read well when they leave third grade, we might be able to prevent lack of progress in school. And if we did that, we might be able to encourage students to stay in school, and to go on to further their educations in whatever fields they show interest. If we all got behind this major effort in education by supporting public policy for education and by becoming mentors to pre-teens, we might be able to provide avenues of success for them which would enhance their self-esteem and help them realize that life holds nearly boundless potential.

What's in it for teens? Another route to adulthood, one that is safer, healthier, more rewarding, one that offers lifelong promise. What's in it for us? If we all got behind this major effort by bringing all of our life experiences, our expertise, and our caring to preteens, well before they are old enough to become sexually active, we could make a difference.

Our support for public education, our mentoring, our role modeling, could reach a young person who is lacking that kind of support. We could give it to them, and we could enjoy the part we would play in their growth and development. What would be good for the teens would be good for society, and what would be good for society, would be good for us.

Why let having a baby be the incentive for young people to make something good of their lives? Let's intervene *before* they create a vulnerable infant. We could feel really good about that.

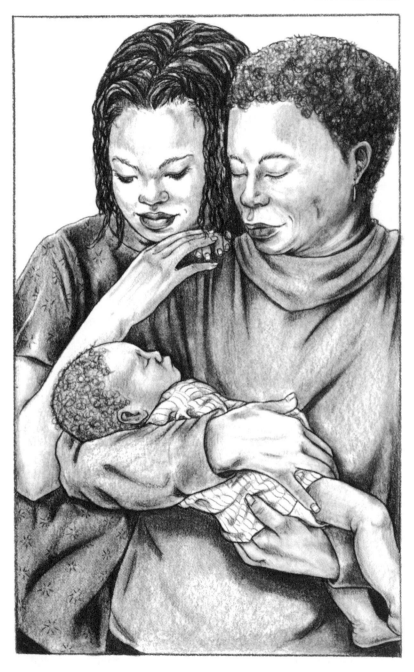

We Can Affect Their Future

We don't all agree on the causes for teenage pregnancy, and we don't all have the same attitudes about teen parents, but we all realize there's a need to address the issue. The statistics support the belief that there are more single teen mothers than there ever have been, but they don't support the notion that it's a new problem.

Teenage childbearing is an old problem. The new part is that there are more *single* teen mothers now. The other new part is that most of them don't believe they would be better off married. Some of us have moral objections to the concept that society accepts single motherhood; others have practical objections.

The research confirms beyond question that children are better off in two-parent families, both psychologically and financially. In order to offer their children a decent standard of living, most families need two incomes. For children to grow up with positive self-esteem, a loving and responsible father in the home is a tremendous asset. A family without a husband/father is frequently a family without the psychological and economic support it needs to thrive. Single teen motherhood presents problems for the teens, for their children, and for the society in which we live. What are we going to do about it?

I propose a solution which could work if every caring person joined in a coalition with every other caring person until the energy was created to form the critical mass that would make the difference. You may want to put this book down right now and say, "She's a dreamer." You'd be right. I am. But I'm in good company.

In Philadelphia in late April of 1997, President Bill Clinton and former President George Bush convened a Presidents' Summit for America's Future, an organization to enlist volunteers from all over America to address the serious social issues we have today. It was a powerful enough idea for General Colin Powell to agree to chair this dream team, and for former Presidents Jimmy Carter and Gerald Ford to join them.[1]

What magnificent dreaming on a massive scale! They must believe, as I do, that the dream has substance, that there are enough concerned people of good will to make a difference.

The researchers, the sociologists, the professionals, and the concerned observers know that something has to happen. But to jump in with band-aid approaches, however well intentioned, would be a waste of our time, effort, resources, and will. Before we recommend possible solutions and courses of action, it's important to ask ourselves what we know about teenage pregnancy. How can we use what we know to make prevention a reality instead of a political statement?

We have been told over and over that the single, most important deterrent to early sex and early pregnancy is a strong, warm relationship between a teen and a caring and responsible adult.[2] We have also been told that teenagers who have poor academic skills and whose parents have limited education are the teens most likely to become pregnant.[3] So we have two key pieces of research on which to build a program. Education and caring adults make a difference. We need to become public lobbyists for education and personal mentors for teens.

As public lobbyists we can be influential with policy-makers by alerting, asking, demanding, or cajoling them to establish priorities for children. We need to let them know that they have a responsibility in teen pregnancy prevention efforts. They must make policy that supports public health, well-being, and education so that teens grow up healthy in mind and body and with positive values.

Having done that, we then turn to ourselves. We become mentors for teens, tutors, role models, friends, who provide nurture of the intangible kind. We take responsibility for their spirits. Our combined efforts will help young people create the confidence, the attitude, the strength of purpose needed to move through adolescence into adulthood, without the encumbrance of too-early parenting.

Policy-makers' public work and our up-close, personal concern will make the difference. By becoming lobbyists and mentors, each of us becomes a trickle of influence. These trickles create a stream which, combined with other streams, could create a river of influence, a confluence which could alter the landscape of society forever.

Creating a Team for Teens

If you like to work alone, contact your local school board, other community leaders, state legislators, and congresspersons. Let them know what you're thinking. Attend meetings where the issues are being discussed. Write letters to the editor.

If you prefer to work with groups, create a **Team for Teens,** gathering together like-minded people in your community. With strength through numbers and united toward a common goal, the Team then makes the contacts, urging school board members and legislators at all levels to make teen pregnancy prevention a priority.

Jim Oliver, teacher at an alternative school in St. Petersburg, Florida, recommends that, in addition to reaching our local policy-makers, we contact people like Jesse Jackson, Newt Gingrich, leaders of the Moral Majority, governors of states, leaders of the Black Caucus in Washington, the President, and tell them to build schools and group homes, not prisons. Tell them to go to work on the circumstances leading to teen pregnancy — poverty, absent fathers, older male predators, lack of achievement in traditional schools — and to develop a local community support system to make life work for these susceptible teens.[4]

Lobby for Education

The researchers stress education. Steve Wulf makes a recommendation for relevant schooling, suggesting that educational institutions create schools better suited to adolescents' developmental needs[5]; ASAP (Advancing Solutions to Adolescent Pregnancy) reports that, to be effective in the prevention of teen pregnancy, we provide education and employment.[6]

During my visits to excellent alternative high schools in Maine and Florida, I saw teachers and administrators making a real difference with teens and their children. The babies were being nurtured and the mothers were being trained by professional care givers. Pregnant and parenting teens were, in addition to being taught traditional high school subjects, exposed to parenting, sex and drug education, and life skills. Most of them had chosen careers and were planning to go on to further

education so they could make a decent living for themselves and their children.[7]

Lobby for continued support for alternative schools for young people like Tammy, Paula, Jenine, and Jewel. Tammy, in a role reversal, got her mother off drugs. When she got pregnant she was fortunate enough to get a second chance in an alternative school.

Tammy, 14: *Mom's straight now. She went to a rehab and finally moved in with my aunt and me. I kept her home, wouldn't let her go out to get drugs. Her fingers were burnt from lighting the stuff. Her face was charred from burns.*

We fought a lot. I'd been driving my aunt's car since I was 12 and Mom wanted me to take her out, but I wouldn't, except to go to church. I finally helped her clean herself up, wash her hair, give up drugs, and now she's healthy. She's 37, and she went back to school to become an R.N. She's graduating this June. I'm getting my second chance in this school so maybe I won't have to go through all she did.

Paula considers her alternative school her family.

Paula, 16: *I feel lucky. My daughter was born with a physical problem, but she got good care. She's on Medicaid and I'm really glad about that. I like being a mom.*

*I go to a good school, she gets good care here, and it's like
a family. At my other school it was bad. There were too many
boys, too much activity, and too much going on to study. I like
it much better with all girls, and I think my life is better now. I
have lots of help with the baby's dad, his mom, and my mom,
and there's a grandma who helps, too. So we're all lucky.*

Jenine and Jewel feel challenged:

Jenine, 16: *I'll make it because I'm the type of person who
makes it if I decide to. For instance, when I was going to high
school, before I got pregnant, if I got to school I did fine. But
I didn't always get there because I was so far ahead of the
other kids that I got bored all the time. So I'd show up now
and then, catch right up with the work, get good grades, and
then quit for awhile to let everybody go ahead. They didn't
give me extra work or anything, but I knew they had to follow
their curriculum, so I just showed up a few days a week.*

*When I moved to this school I read a lot on my own. I
decided that I was going to find out more about my Aztec
Indian heritage, and I researched that. I was so excited when
I found out that my great-grandfather was one of the original
settlers in this area, and I found some of the old diaries. In
this school they challenge me.*

Jewel, 17: *I ran away, but went back home to my mom when I
was eight months pregnant. She said the one thing I couldn't
do was just sit around, and that I had to choose either work
or school. By then I knew a lot about work and figured it was
time to finish school. So I came to this school for teenage
mothers.*

*My baby is six weeks old now. She gets wonderful care in
the nursery here, and I'm going to graduate in a few months.
I'm smart and it isn't hard for me to do the work. I think*

maybe that was the problem with school before. It completely lost me. I'd ask questions a lot, but the teachers were too busy with 40 other kids to bother with me, and they just gave me more worksheets to do. This school deals with stuff that matters to me, like how to take care of my daughter, and how to take care of myself.

Michael Epstein, a counselor in an alternative school in Bradenton, Florida, recognizes the value of alternative schools, but also believes that social policy needs to be changed in a broader way. Starting with middle school age, he says, we have to start treating kids as older than we have been doing. Give them respect. Recognize effort. Redo the grading system and appeal to different learning styles. Offer the finest sex and drug education available. Reach all kids. Give them a fighting chance. If their homes aren't offering emotional support, then we have to do it for them.[8]

Innovation in Education

Lobby for good programs like the innovative examples below. Education comes in many guises.

Gregg Chappel, the director of Rebound Youth Services in Sarasota, Florida, teaches carpentry in his classroom, not just for the purpose of making things, but to improve teens' self-esteem and to illustrate the value of work. It's a classroom in a second chance school for dropouts or "kickouts" from other schools.[9]

Another of these "second chance" schools, called Character House, is designed for female juvenile delinquents, some of them pregnant. Under the auspices of the Young Men's Christian Association (YMCA), this is the first of two such homes for girls aged 14 to 18.

Most have been sexually abused, have been in trouble with the law, and have been ordered to live in this home. Along with counseling, educational and vocational training, and parenting skills, the young women are being taught responsibility. It's up to them to master the behavior and attitudes which will earn their way out, according to a spokesman for the Department of Juvenile Justice.[10]

The Real Life Cost Model (RLCM), developed by Dr. Brenda Jarmon at Florida State University, holds promise for a new generation of teens. Her program educates middle school students about the real costs of unintended pregnancy. Dr. Jarmon, a single mother at the age of 15, recalls being thrown out of the house she shared with the father of her children and landing on her face in a mud puddle. "With one baby on my hip and one in my belly, I asked myself, what am I doing?" Her life's work with teenage pregnancy prevention began that day.[11]

In my own community of Sarasota, Florida, inspired by President Clinton's call that all students leave third grade being able to read at or above grade level, I designed an alternative approach to reading and enlisted the help of friends. A group of us, all retired professionals, piloted this model for ten below-grade-level fourth and fifth graders. We worked one semester, one period a week, with the expectation that we might see a little progress. To our delight, standardized pre- and post-testing documented a two- to three-year growth in reading in nine of the ten students.[12]

A program can involve the full resources of a major university. Harvard University, assessing the needs of the children in the United States, recently started a project on children and schooling. In addition to its focus on questions of public policy such as the question of the role of schools in society, it is now offering new courses that will deal with issues of adoption, education, sexuality, identity, delinquency, abuse and neglect, and poverty.[13]

The interesting part is that it's not the size or the amount of money that leads to success. It's the vision, the relevance, and the commitment of the sponsors. Most of these programs could be replicated in every community.

Group Homes Needed

Lobby for group homes, and a change in current housing law, because without the security of safe shelter, teen parents have difficulty learning. As others have said, cognitive learning cannot occur in a state of affective disorder.

These homes provide teen mothers and at-risk teens with a haven, a sense of family, and the role models they need to thrive. They cannot move out of family homes and live on their own because the current law requires an age minimum of 18 before a person can get help from HUD for independent housing.

Kathleen Witton, a counselor at an alternative high school, Bradenton, Florida, argues that there has to be some leeway for kids under 18 to be able to leave home when they need to.[14] Their moms take the welfare check and leave their own babies with the girls and their babies. Even though these girls are younger, they need safe shelter. They have no choices when they're stuck in abusive or neglectful home situations. We have to provide shelter and emotional support so they can raise productive, independent children.

Joyce lives in a group home where she has pulled her life together:

Joyce, 16: *I'll graduate high school and then go on to college. I want to work with children. I want to be a mental health worker, maybe a pediatrician or a psychiatrist. I want to be in a position to help them and to show them how to do the right thing.*

I have a teacher now who really cares. I want to be like her. I know you can do it if you say you can do it and if you believe in yourself. I have been through a lot in my life. I dropped out of school because I thought it was no use, but I pulled my life together. These people in the home I live in and this school have given me the opportunity to make it, and I will.

Gail found safety among friends and adults who care about her:

Gail, 17: *We were in foster homes, and got kicked out of one after another, and each time I went to a new school. I can't count the number of schools I've been in. Last year, when I got pregnant, I got kicked out of another foster home. I dropped out of school entirely, and this time I was placed in a special home for pregnant teens and school dropouts.*

I go to this special school, too, and for the first time in my life I feel safe. I'm doing well here. I'm even on the honor roll. And my baby is in the nursery here while I go to classes. When we both go home I have adults who care about us and friends like me who are taking care of their babies and going to school. My life has never been better. My baby is precious, and I'm so happy to have her.

Ginger has been accepted:

Ginger, 13: *Mom was so upset when I told her I was pregnant that I decided to move out. I live in a group home now, with 15 girls and 12 babies. We go to this alternative school, and the babies are cared for here during the day. I take care of her when I go home.*

I'm happy and I do well in school. I have my first best friend here. I'm the youngest mother in the home, but they all treat me well, just as if I'm their age. We act the same and have the same responsibilities.

Updating the Laws

Lobby for a change in the laws governing teen mothers and fathers.

According to Michael Epstein, we need new laws about the rights and responsibilities of the father. We need to deal with the emancipation of the teenage mom. We have to work on the economic and social issues of providing shelter, schooling, and jobs. We need to deal with absent fathers, sexual abuse, poverty — all conditions which predispose teens to too-early parenting. We have to do things differently so teens can make better choices.[15]

Andy Tartler, a social worker at an alternative high school, agrees that we need to recognize that teen parents have adult problems. We are depending on old-fashioned notions to solve new-fashioned problems, he says. We have to enforce child support laws, and those concerning older men who prey on young girls. We have to teach these girls how to deal with government agencies.[16]

Our laws no longer fit today's circumstances in which one single young mother is head of the family. We must do a better job of answering these questions and solving this problem or

these kids' kids will come to haunt us. Our continued failure to
deal with this problem is costing us now and will cost us more
each day. These babies will not go away.

Changing Workplace Policies

Lobby for a change of policies in the workplace. Working
mothers need flex time for their families.

Constance H. Buchanan, Associate Dean of the Harvard
Divinity School, did a sociological analysis of welfare reform.
She writes, "By reforming welfare, by requiring poor single
mothers to move into the paid labor force and discouraging
births to unmarried women, both presidential candidates (1996)
positioned themselves to claim moral leadership in addressing
the nation's values crisis. But for both, this claim will be false.

"They have helped make what should have been a debate
about how to eliminate poverty, not just reduce the welfare rolls,
into a diagnosis of the cause of the nation's moral woes. Mean-
while, the nation's real values crisis is taking place unaddressed
in the structure of mainstream American life, not at its margin
among the vulnerable population of welfare mothers easy to
characterize as lacking personal values.

"The move to reform welfare is actually about bringing the
nation's expectation of poor mothers up to date with the changed
cultural norm for all American mothers. In this country a 'good'
mother tends no longer to be one who stays at home, but rather
one who is employed.

"This leaves unaddressed the real source of many of the
country's woes — the erosion of the bonds of family and community mutuality and obligation, which society depends on. This
erosion is taking place across lines of race, ethnicity, and class.
The unpaid labor of weaving and sustaining these bonds has
traditionally been women's work. But now economic necessity
has driven 48 percent of mothers into the paid labor force,

sharply decreasing the resources society is putting into this labor.

"Paradoxically, we need to look forward, not backward, if we are to sustain values that Americans care about and the nation depends on. Political leaders capable of addressing this moral challenge will envision new ways to help us sustain eroding nonmarket values by reconfiguring the work-family-community nexus," she concluded.[17]

Importance of Personal Involvement

If, as lobbyists, we move the policy-makers to support these changes, why do we still need to get involved at the personal level? I believe we can offer another dimension. Many young people today, through a combination of economic, social, and political circumstances, are being deprived of the close adult nurturing they need to develop their sense of conscience, responsibility, good citizenship, and self-esteem. As mentors, we can fill that role.

Why mentor? Mentor to be a role model, to nurture, to help teens resist negative peer pressure, to share experiences, to befriend, and to be companions to lonely children.

Jim Oliver remembers Wren, one of his students. "Take Wren as an example," he said. "Her mother was doing drugs, and Wren had no solid relationship with her parents. It's easier for kids to give in to negative peer pressure if there isn't a solid relationship with parents. Kids will respond to peer pressure more easily if they feel parents are not taking good care of them.

"A strong, loving relationship with a parent is the best defense against negative peer pressure. Having none, Wren took the route of the crowd and got into sex when she was only 13. Now she's a mother at 14.

"In my neighborhood," he went on, "the basic elements of self-esteem that are needed are security, a purpose in life, goals, belonging to a proactive organization, identity, education, and information. Most adolescents live in fear that the world will end in their lifetime. Is there a future with AIDS, natural disasters, nuclear accidents?

"Peer pressure would be minimal if they had all of the above. The schools need to give them real information about sex and drugs so they stop believing the myths and partial truths they hear at home. They need to know about nutrition, health and safety, and they need to recognize an old wives' tale when they hear it."[18]

Referring to the research which says that the best defense against negative peer pressure is a loving, caring, and responsible adult, I believe mentors could bring that resistance to the lives   of teens.

Mentoring Values

Mentor to help establish the standards and values we feel are missing today.

Pat Hartstein, director of an alternative middle and high school in St. Petersburg, Florida, believes it's up to us. She says, "Society can't be run by the buck alone. We have to go back to standards. We need standards in schools, in churches, in government, in public places, and in the home. We have to have high expectations for our young people, and the whole culture has to work on it. Material things are what count now. That's what young people see and hear. We have to change that.

"We have to do something about sex, abuse, and violence in our culture. We have to work on the media in general, particularly TV, magazines, and the movies. When our whole culture decides it's time to stress human values, and time to make having material things less important, then we'll begin to make a dent in the problems society has now. These girls are just a symptom of a bigger disease. It's up to us."[19]

Are Pat and the rest of us right in lamenting the loss of

standards and values? George Soros, financier and philanthropist, has an interesting analysis. He writes about our problem in an "open society," the name he gives to our democratic form of government.

Soros says we enjoy the freedoms democracy gives us, we cherish the right for a person to pursue his economic self-interest as far as it can take him, we appreciate the rights to worship or not as we choose and to manage our households as we please. But, he adds, without a set of moral principles which are deeply rooted in tradition, religion, and culture to guide us, we are threatened by these very freedoms.

We had these principles once, according to Soros, but the morals of the marketplace have taken over. Market values have undermined and overtaken the more traditional values system, and this is the cause of the current breakdown in our society.[20]

I think this explanation goes a long way toward helping us understand why we are where we are, and why the issue of how to deal with teenage pregnancy arouses such passion at all points in the political/social/religious/economic continuum of beliefs. The "survival of the fittest" philosophy has become so much a value in society that we have lost our balance. As mentors, as personal examples, however, we can provide the stability teens need and help them plan the course for their lives.

Changing Roles of Mothers

We can mentor to provide the bonds of family and community, to fill in for absent parents, more prevalent today than in the past.

As Soros and Buchanan point out, in keeping with our materialistic, market-driven values, we have redefined the notion of a "good" mother. When I was a young mother, my role was clear. College educated, ambitious, I was nevertheless expected to stay home and take care of my husband and our children. Society

valued my ability to cook, to clean, and to nurture. I, not in-
trigued by the values of cooking and cleaning, did value the
opportunity to nurture. I look back and see what a privilege it
was to do that. But I was itchy.

When I decided, in 1963 at the age of 38, that my children
were old enough, my husband was capable enough, and I was
sorely in need of mental stimulation, I went back to school. From
there I became a teacher, working part-time at first, then full-
time until I retired 30 years later.

My own family supported me all the way, but in our circle of
friends there were those who were appalled that I had become a
wage-earner. What was wrong with my husband? Wasn't he
capable of making a living any more? Was something wrong
with our marriage? Why was I abandoning my children?

The war, the economy, and the birth control pill set the stage
for women to join the workforce, and the mores changed. Many
of today's mothers don't have the opportunity to stay home and
nurture their children. Women, many of them single mothers, are
now in the labor force in numbers almost equal to men. No
longer frowned upon, work for women has become a fiscal
necessity. How else would families manage? The results of two-
parent absence are all around us, as poor single mothers, without
the resources to provide quality care for their children, leave
them to be nurtured by television, slightly older siblings, an
occasional neighbor, or no one.

The Carnegie Council recommends that parents re-engage
themselves with their children, with the help of family-friendly
policies by employers.[20] As we go to press, Congress and the
President are debating the viability of time off instead of over-
time for workers. The need for parental time to care for children
is recognized, but we're far from implementing it. Mentors can
make a difference by being temporary parental substitutes to
preteens and teens whose mother and/or father are working.

Modeling Relationship Skills

Mentor to help teens see the values of solid, enduring relationships with the opposite sex.

Nanette Dizney, director of an alternative high school in Bradenton, Florida, was a single mom, the child of a single mother. "Having a single mom as a parent leaves a lasting impression on a child. That's why we have to stop the cycle. Today's single teen moms had single moms themselves. When you're a single mom you've got to turn the negative to the positive. You have to deny that you're not good enough. You have to feel good enough. It's not okay to think you don't have what it takes.

"An attorney friend told me I couldn't make it when I, a single mother, had three kids and wanted to go back to school. No man was going to tell me what I couldn't do. I went back, got the degree, and a few more. This is what we have to teach young women. They can make it and we're going to help them."[22]

In addition to better legislation and enforcement of existing laws to stop the problem of male predators and sexual abuse, we need much better adult role models. Right now sex outside of a committed relationship is accepted by many movie stars, athletes, TV stars, even government officials. The girls see this and think it's okay for them, too.

We also have to make sure that the current group of babies born to teenage mothers are cared for so they will be healthy children, not sick children. It takes a generation to make a change. We need earlier intervention and better education. These girls are not getting pregnant because they want sex; they are getting pregnant because they want love, attention, recognition, understanding, affection. They need love. We can let them know we love them.

Yes, it's up to us. Mentors can be the standard-setters, the deliverers of values, the role models, the support systems.

How Do We Mentor?

A variety of interventions can work. We can mentor as part of a program, or as an individual. Success depends on commitment.

Let's look at what's working now before we take off in a dozen directions to invent everything new. I've gathered examples of innovative programs that are making a difference. Some are the result of one person's vision. This person works alone, or with a small group of colleagues or friends, to reach out to teens. Others are the result of major changes in a community, guided and directed by public policy, staffed by large numbers of caring and responsible adults.

What interests me is that it isn't the size of the project, or even the amount of money spent on it. It's the philosophy, the vision, the determination, and the energy behind it that makes for success.

"Top Cop Hits the Streets," the headline read. What's going on, I wondered, as I read about Police Chief Daniel Thorpe of Bradenton, Florida. Here was Chief Thorpe, sitting on a chair in a busy neighborhood park. "The Chief's In," the sign in front of him announced. The neighbors, who normally would be surrounded by drug pushers and troublemakers, had access to the Police Chief, just to talk. So successful are the Chief's efforts, the drug dealers complain about him.

He has also organized neighborhood crime watch, bicycle patrols, and police walking the beat. He's a role model for the children, he knows what's going on, they like him, and he is making a difference.[23]

That's a good story, we say, but where do you find someone like that? In Norfolk, Virginia, Principal Herman Clark of the Bowling Park School has organized his whole school around "surrogate parenthood." Here children and their parents are part of a caring community. The school provides parent educators to pregnant women, so they begin caring for their children in utero.

The school has taken on the business of parenthood in the absence of fathers, and often of mothers who are drug addicted, alcoholic, depressed, or otherwise unable to cope.[24] Can it work? It is working in 47 states, to which it spread because of its success in one school. Principal Clark made a difference.

In Jacksonville, Florida, the Recreation Department doesn't wait for the teens to come to them. They go to the 23 middle schools every afternoon where they provide games, sports, crafts, trips, job training, and tutoring.

In Cheyenne, Wyoming, the Botanic Garden, a conservatory that grows food for low-income food kitchens, provides plants for city parks. The work of planting them and caring for them is done by at-risk teens who are learning responsibility and the value of work while they enjoy the appreciation of the communities in which they work.[25]

You may say, "But I'm not a top cop or an educator or a recreation leader." Don't worry. Good mentoring doesn't depend on a particular skill. A mentor needs only to care, and to be willing to share a part of himself or herself. You can make a real difference in whatever role you play with these teens.

If your skill is to listen, then listen; if your skill is to talk, then talk; if it is to teach, then teach; if it is to provide work, then provide; if it is to model skills; then model; if it is to make a holiday and create a tradition, then make it; if it is to show love in any number of ways, then show it to them and to their babies.

You may be a good storyteller who can talk with them about your history, your traditions. You may be a teen who can participate as a model by asking younger teens to walk in your footsteps in order to see the reality of teen pregnancy and parenting.

If you are active in an organization, mobilize it to create new opportunities, the more exciting, the better. Convince your group to talk with other groups for the purpose of joining forces. The

Florida Summit,[26] the Impact Study,[27] the ASAP Report,[28] and the National Campaign to Prevent Teen Pregnancy[29] all recommend community-based coalitions as forces in the prevention of teen pregnancy.

You *Can* Change Lives

Whatever you do, if you break through the hopelessness, the despair, the emotional lethargy, the lack of motivation, the low self-esteem of children who are feeling neglected, you may keep a preteen from becoming a teenage parent. If the teen is already pregnant or parenting, you have an opportunity to reach teen parents so that they, and their children, have a chance. An additional benefit may be that, as adults and teens get to know each other at the personal level, they will see people, not stereotypes, individuals with hopes and dreams not too different from their own.

Think about this. If every preteen and teen who needs an interested, attentive adult has one, in whatever area suits the pair best, we will have gone a long way toward sustaining or restoring self-esteem, hope, and courage to this generation of potential teen moms or teen dads. How many said that their pregnancy saved their lives, for now they had a good school, good people, and hope?

If we read the teen stories carefully, we see the same lack over and over. They needed a mom to listen, a dad to understand. They needed direction, limits, attention, time. For any number of reasons these things were missing, and when someone came along to say, "I love you" or "I want you," they thought, "Here is love." Sex became love. Or they had no choice in the matter. They were abused, raped, emotionally disabled. Pregnancy, though not sought, frequently followed.

Why do so many teens keep their children? This is a chance for love, they think. This is the chance to be special, to be

needed. They don't see beyond that because they are young, naive, inexperienced, and emotionally needy.
They told us what they need. Let's give it to them.

My personal belief is that we, as a society, must solve this problem, not just because it is humane to care for children and their children, but because it is the intelligent, pragmatic thing to do if we are to save our society as we know it. If we do not find ways to break this cycle of poverty, despair and dependency, we will all suffer for it, not just the teens and their children. We cannot continue to widen the gap between the haves and the have-nots, between the middle/upper-middle classes and the underclass, without putting all classes at risk.

This generation of children being born to single teen mothers must grow up educated, self-sufficient, and with positive self-esteem or this problem will multiply to numbers yet undreamed of. No city will be safe; no suburb will be safe; our socio-political system will suffer disruption we have experienced only sporadically up to now. Every home will need an armed guard, a situation common to those who can afford them in some South American countries. We are living in a fantasy world if we think this problem will just go away.

If we feel the price is too high, if we close our eyes and turn our backs on it, it will sneak up on us as we sleep. The facilities of our cities, our schools, our hospitals, and our housing will face even more critical problems than they do today. The violence in our communities will only accelerate.

If we still need a wake-up call, let this image be it. We must, right now, choose active, informed involvement, all of us together, in the solutions to this problem. If we don't choose to do it for the sake of the teen parents and their children, then let's do it for the sake of our own children or for ourselves.

They told us what they need. Let's give it to them.

Afterword

This book was conceived by the spark of my mother's love and the sensitivity of Professor Bob McGrath. It was born after hard labor during which I learned who teen mothers were and how they felt about their new roles as mothers. It was delivered through the insight of Jeanne Warren Lindsay of Morning Glory Press. And now this baby of mine is about to go out into the real world. Just as at the moments when we launch our children into the world — the first day of kindergarten, the first overnight visit away from home, the first day of college, the first day of a new job — we feel pride that the child is ready to go it alone, fear that we may not have done a good enough job, and a pang of regret that we have to let go. *Teen Moms: The Pain and the Promise* has been my constant companion for over two years. Now I have to let it go. It is yours. Did I do a good job? Will it make its way into your heart and mind?

If you had a negative view of teen parenthood and are moved to a new understanding, it has been successful. If you have not been working with young people and are moved to make a contribution of your time, energy, and expertise to become a mentor to a preteen or a teen, it has been successful. If you have not been involved in organizations at the political, social, religious or school level and are moved to work with your legislature, your local school, your organization, or your religious group to find a way to affect teen and preteen education, it has been successful.

As I finish this page, turn on the printer, and get up to stretch, I once again feel my mother's presence. If she were living today and I could ask her the question, "Mamatchka, what do children need to grow strong and healthy?" I am sure her answer would be, "Love and education." She'd approve of the course of action I have suggested. Quite probably, she was suggesting it all along.

Appendix

Description
of Interview Group

In the course of the two years I spent gathering material and researching the data for this book, I made 253 contacts with fifty pregnant teens and teen mothers. I interviewed them as individuals, in small groups, in large groups, and by questionnaire. When I finished writing up interviews, I enlisted the help of two large reading classes in alternative high schools and asked them to critique the stories, making sure the case studies came from different areas and that the names were fictitious. I asked them to rate interest, relevance, and readability as criteria for selection. Their responses aided me in selecting passages used in the book.

Extrapolating from the data gathered in individual interviews, the ethnic mix was 56 percent Caucasian, 29 percent African American, 8 percent Hispanic, 6 percent racially mixed. The data gathered from all contacts revealed that the young women were aged 11 to 18; the males 13 to 53. The majority of pregnancies occurred at age 15 or older; the majority of the fathers were 18 or older. Individual pairings substantiated the research that in the majority of cases, the younger the female, the older the male.

Becoming a Lobbyist

If you feel that what you have read in this book is important for people in power to hear, please let your legislators know your feelings regarding what needs to be done about and for single, teenage mothers. Here is a letter I sent to President and Mrs. Clinton expressing my views. Feel free to use any part or parts of it to convey your concerns. A letter to the President, your Congressmen or Congresswomen, your Senators, your Governor, and your school board members could go a long way toward raising their consciousness about this issue.

President Bill Clinton and Ms. Hilary Rodham Clinton
The White House
Washington, DC 20500
Fax: 202-456-2461

Dear President and Ms. Clinton:
    What are we going to do about single, teenage mothers? I know this topic is of tremendous importance to you. It is so important to me that I have spent the last two years interviewing

young women aged 13 to 18, representative of lower-middle and middle class Caucasians, Blacks, Hispanics, and Native Americans, for a book called *Teen Moms: The Pain and the Promise.*

These interviews took place in alternative high schools where the babies were cared for in professional nurseries while the mothers completed their high school education. In the course of these interviews and group discussions, I gleaned the following information which I hope you will have the opportunity to read. Here is what they say:

1. *They are working very hard to finish high school and raise their babies, but they would gladly hold jobs if the law allowed it.*

2 *They are ashamed to be receiving welfare checks and food stamps, but they cannot survive without them.*

3. *Thirteen-, fourteen-, and fifteen-year-olds are too young to be allowed to work.*

4. *Those who can work, do, but those who cannot try to earn money by babysitting, doing errands, etc.*

5. *Most are raising their children without help from the father of the child, either financial, physical, or emotional.*

6. *Most have come from abusive homes in which they have suffered sexual abuse, physical abuse, and verbal abuse.*

7. *Many, some when as young as four years old, have been responsible for raising younger siblings alone because the single mother was out working, or was an alcoholic, drug addict and/or prostitute.*

8. *They feel they are being better mothers to their children than their mothers were to them because they are learning how to be good parents in this school setting and because they are not dropouts like their mothers were.*

9. *They were turned off by the regular high school they attended, and some dropped out.*

10. *They feel lucky they got pregnant because it got them out of the wrong school for them. It got them away from the drugs, alcoholism, and gang activities they were into before.*

11. They plan to finish high school and go on to higher education so they can be well-trained and make enough money to take care of their children independently of a man, a parent, or the state or federal government.

12. They worry a lot about being good mothers, about society's prejudice against them and view of them as "trash." They worry about the world they live in and their ability to keep their children alive and off drugs.

In view of these insights, I respectfully recommend the following course of action to you:

1. Work with the schools to provide earlier intervention programs in elementary schools so the needs of these children are met earlier.

2. Enlist neighborhood groups of all types to guarantee safe environments for young children in their formative years.

3. Provide group homes and group schooling for girls who are being molested by their families.

4. Provide job opportunities for girls under the age of 16, particularly girls who have become mothers.

5. Continue to support alternative middle schools and high schools for these young women and their children.

6. Support research and reporting on the societal problems these young women face, i.e. rape, incest, older male predators, poverty, gangs, drugs, AIDS, so that the public image of them as "sinners" can be changed.

7. Support "Teams for Teens," the mentoring program described in the book.

Thank you for your attention.

Yours very truly,

Evelyn Lerman
Sarasota, Florida
February, 1997

Research Citations

Chapter 1. Start with Statistics — The Realities

1. Abrna, J. C., Chandra, A., Mosher, W. D., et al. "Fertility, Family Planning, and Women's Health." *The 1995 National Survey of Family Growth.* Hyattsville, MD: National Center for Health Statistics, *Vital Health Stat 23(19), 1997, excerpts.*

2. *Sex and America's Teenagers.* New York: The Alan Guttmacher Institute, 1994, p.19.

3. Ibid.

4. Ibid., p. 19, p. 55.

5. Ibid., p. 52.

6. Ibid., p. 51.

7. Centers for Disease Control and Prevention. Huntsville, AL: *Monthly Vital Statistics Report,* August 23, 1996, p. 1.

8. *Sex and America's Teenagers,* op. cit., p. 4.

9. Musick, Judith S. *Young, Poor, and Pregnant.* New Haven: Yale University Press, 1993, p. 44.

10. *Sex and America's Teenagers,* op. cit., p. 30.

11. Navarro, Mireya. "Teen-Age Mothers Viewed as Abused by Older

11. Navarro, Mireya. "Teen-Age Mothers Viewed as Abused by Older Men." New York: *New York Times,* May 19, 1996, p. 19.

12. *Sex and America's Teenagers,* op. cit., p. 62.

13. *Kids Count Data Book.* Baltimore, MD: Annie E. Casey Foundation, 1997, p. 21.

14. *Sex and America's Teenagers,* op. cit., p. 4.

15. Ibid., p. 22.

16. Males, Mike A. *The Scapegoat Generation.* Monroe, ME: Common Courage Press, 1996, p. 17.

17. *A Prospectus for the National Campaign to Prevent Teen Pregnancy.* Kean, Hon. Thomas H., Chair. Washington, DC.

18. Congressional Research Service. The Library of Congress: *CRS Report for Congress,* August 23, 1996.

19. *Sex and America's Teenagers,* op. cit., p. 45.

20. Ibid., p. 5.

21. Centers for Disease Control, op. cit., p. 1.

22. *Sex and America's Teenagers,* op. cit., p. 9.

23. *Kids Count Data Book,* op. cit., p. 8.

24. Luker, Kristin. *Dubious Conceptions.* Cambridge, MA: Harvard University Press, 1996, p. 103.

25. *Sex and America's Teenagers,* op. cit., pp. 12, 21, 23.

Chapter 2 Why Have Sex So Early?

1. Anderson, Gael. Bradenton, FL: Interviews, February, 1996.

2. Males, Mike. "The Determinants of First Sex by Age 14." *PSAY Network,* March, 1996, p. 11.

3. Males, Mike A. *The Scapegoat Generation.* Monroe, ME: Common Courage Press, 1996, p. 63.

4. Ibid., p. 11.

5. Musick, Judith S. "Poverty and Teen Pregnancy: Implications for Programs." Rutgers, NJ: *Family Life Matters,* Spring, 1995, p. 1.

6. *Sex and America's Teenagers.* New York: The Alan Guttmacher Institute, 1994, p. 1.

7. Edelman, Hope. *Motherless Daughters.* New York: Dell, Bantam Doubleday, 1974, p. 10.

8. Musick, Judith S. *Young, Poor, and Pregnant.* New Haven, CT:

Yale University Press, 1993, p. 75.

9. Dizney, Nanette. Bradenton, FL: Interviews, February, 1996.

10. Schilling, Max. "Hidden Factors in Teenage Childbearing." Tallahassee, FL: Florida Department of Education, June, 1996, p. 2.

11. Males, *The Scapegoat Generation*, op. cit., p. 95.

12. Ibid., p. 67.

13. Klein, Joe. "Public Lives," New York: *Newsweek*, April 29, 1996.

14. Males, *The Scapegoat Generation*, op. cit., p. 56.

15. Sweeney, Camille. "Portrait of the American Child." New York: *New York Times Magazine*, October 18, 1996, p. 2.

16. Epstein, Michael and Tartler, Andy. Bradenton and St. Petersburg, FL: Interviews, April/May, 1996.

17. Boyer, Debra. "Adolescent Pregnancy: The Role of Sexual Abuse." Huntsville, AL: *NRCCSA News*, December, 1995, p. 3.

18. Navarro, Mireya. "Teen-Age Mothers Viewed as Abused by Older Men." New York: *New York Times*, May 19, 1996, p. 1.

19. Males, *The Scapegoat Generation*, op. cit., p. 17.

20. Klein, Joe. "The Predator Problem." *Newsweek*, April 29, 1996, p. 32.

21. Edelman, op. cit., p. 140, 145-146.

22. Dorrell, Larry D. "A Future at Risk: Children Having Children." Warrensburg, MO: *Clearing House*, March, 1994, p. 2.

23. Oliver, Jim. St. Petersburg, FL: Interviews, April/May, 1996.

24. Dash, Leon. *When Children Want Children*. New York: William Morrow & Co., 1989, p. 34.

25. Moran, Bea. Bradenton, FL: Interviews, February, 1996.

26. Dash, op. cit., p. 15.

27. *Sex and America's Teenagers*, op. cit., p. 36.

28. Schilling, Max: phone conversation, December 13, 1996.

29. *Sex and America's Teenagers*, op. cit., p. 11.

30. Ibid., p. 7.

31. Musick, *Young, Poor, and Pregnant*. op. cit., pp. 53-54.

32. Lerman, Evelyn. Conversations, 1994-1996.

33. *Sex and America's Teenagers*, op. cit., p. 7.

34. Males, *The Scapegoat Generation*, op. cit., p. 63.

35. Moore, Kristin, ed. *Facts at a Glance*. Washington, DC: Child Trends, Inc., Jan., 1996, p. 44.

36. Ibid.

37. Usdansky, M. L. "Single Motherhood: Stereotypes vs. Statistics." New York: *New York Times*, February 11, 1996, p. 4.

38. *Sex and America's Teenagers*, op. cit., p. 52.

39. Musick, op. cit., p. 9.

40. *Sex and America's Teenagers*, op. cit., p. 5.

Chapter 3. Teen Moms' Feelings About Men

1. Musick, Judith S. *Young, Poor, and Pregnant*. New Haven, CT: Yale University Press, 1993, p. 95.

2. Boyer, Debra. "Adolescent Pregnancy: The Role of Sexual Abuse." Huntsville, AL: *NRCCSA News*, December, 1995, p. 3.

3. Musick, op. cit., pp. 101-102.

4. Males, Mike A. *The Scapegoat Generation*. Monroe, ME: Common Courage Press, 1996, p. 19.

5. Kamiya, Katherine A. *Teen Pregnancy Summit Report*. Tallahassee, FL: FDDC, 1994, p. 5.

6. *Sex and America's Teenagers*. New York: The Alan Guttmacher Institute, 1994, p. 53.

7. Males, op. cit., p. 68.

8. *Kids Count Data Book*. Baltimore, MD: Annie E. Casey Foundation, 1997, p. 21.

9. *Sex and America's Teenagers*, op. cit., p. 5.

10. Ibid., p. 33.

11. Ibid., pp. 23-24.

12. "Invincible Kids." Washington, DC: *U.S. News and World Report*, Nov. 11, 1996, pp. 63-71.

13. Musick, op. cit., pp. 168-169.

14. Pipher, Mary. *Reviving Ophelia: Saving the Souls of Adolescent Girls*. New York: Ballantine Books, 1995, pp. 117-118.

Chapter 4. The Meaning of Motherhood

1. Musick, Judith S. *Young, Poor, and Pregnant*. New Haven, CT: Yale University Press, 1993, p. 180-181.

2. Ibid., p. 186.

3. Males, Mike A. *The Scapegoat Generation.* Monroe, ME: Common Courage Press, 1996, p. 11.

4. Luker, Kristin. *Dubious Conceptions.* Cambridge, MA: Harvard University Press, 1996, p. 107.

5. *Teenage Pregnancy.* Arlington, VA: American Association of School Administrators; and New York: Association of Junior Leagues, Inc., 1988, p. 3.

6. *Kids Count Data Book.* Baltimore, MD: Annie E. Casey Foundation, 1997, p. 16.

7. *Kids Count Data Book,* Baltimore, MD: Annie E. Casey Foundation, 1996, p. 7.

8. *Teenage Pregnancy,* op. cit. p. 3.

9. Joe, Ronald, Chair. *Impact Of Teen Pregnancy In Florida.* Tallahassee, FL, University of Central Florida, FEECWG, 1995, p. 18.

10. Males. op. cit., p. 119.

11. Luker. op. cit. p. 129.

12. Edelman, Hope. *Motherless Daughters.* New York: Dell, Bantam Doubleday, 1974, p. 43.

13. Musick. op. cit., p. 181.

Chapter 5. The Worries Come Swiftly

1. Lerman, Evelyn. Waterville, ME: Survey. September, 1995, conducted by Sharon Abrams.

2. Luker, Kristin. *Dubious Conceptions.* Cambridge, MA: Harvard University Press, 1996, p. 129.

3. Kamiya, Katherine A. *Teen Pregnancy Summit Report.* Tallahassee, FL: FDDC, 1994, p. 7.

4. Pipher, Mary. *Reviving Ophelia: Saving the Souls of Adolescent Girls.* New York: Ballantine Books, 1995, p. 83.

5. *Teenage Pregnancy.* Arlington, VA: American Association of School Administrators; and New York: Association of Junior Leagues, Inc., 1988, p. 2.

6. Ibid., pp. 4, 6.

7. *Kids Count Data Book.* Baltimore, MD: Annie E. Casey Foundation, 1996, p. 21.

8. Males, Mike A. *The Scapegoat Generation*. Monroe, ME: Common Courage Press, 1996, p. 161.

9. *Maine Kids Count*. Augusta, ME: Maine Children's Alliance, 1995-96, p. 15.

10. *Sex and America's Teenagers*. New York: The Alan Guttmacher Institute. 1994, pp. 9, 3.

11. *Teenage Pregnancy*, op. cit., p. 2.

Chapter 6. Feelings About Welfare and Independence

1. "Clinton Announces Teen Welfare Plan." Sarasota, FL: *Herald-Tribune*, May 5, 1996, p. A5.

2. Buchanan, Constance H. "Welfare Is Not the Problem." Boston, MA: *Boston Globe*, July 7, 1996, p. A23.

3. Jacoby, Jeff. "Welfare Catastrophe?" Boston, MA: *Boston Globe*, August 6, 1996, p. 12.

4. Goldsmith, Steve. "Revamping Welfare: Building Lives." New York: *New York Times*, August 4, 1996, p. 15.

5. Bennet, James. "Clinton Seeks Help on Proposal over Welfare." Sarasota, FL: *Herald-Tribune*, January 10, 1997, p. 7.

6. Kilborn, Peter. "States Crafting Ambitious Plans." New York: *New York Times*. December 16, 1996, p. A1.

7. Hartstein, Pat. St. Petersburg, FL: Interviews. Fall, 1996.

8. Kuttner, Robert. "A Damaging Welfare Bill." Boston: *Boston Globe*, August 10, 1996, p. A11.

9. Luker, Kristin. *Dubious Conceptions*. Cambridge, MA: Harvard University Press, 1996, p. 126.

10. Kilborn, Peter T. "Welfare All Over the Map." New York: *New York Times*, December 8, 1996, p. 3.

11. Males, Mike A. *The Scapegoat Generation*. Monroe, ME: Common Courage Press, 1996, p. 67.

12. "New Study's Findings Contradict Welfare Stereotype." Sarasota, FL: AP, *Herald-Tribune*, September 17, 1996, p. A3.

13. *Kids Count Data Book*. Baltimore, MD: Annie E. Casey Foundation, 1996, p. 5.

14. *Teenage Pregnancy*. Arlington, VA: American Association of School Administrators; and New York: Association of Junior Leagues, Inc., 1988, p. 1.

15. Kilborn, "States Crafting Ambitious Plans." op. cit., p. A1.

16. *Congressional Quarterly Weekly Report.* Washington, DC: Library of Congress. August 3, 1996, p. 2190.

17. Ibid., p. 2192.

18. Maxwell, Bill. "Those Who Criticize Can Contribute," *Sarasota Herald-Tribune,* Sept. 9, 1996.

Chapter 7. Changed Lives — The Pain and the Promise

1. Musick, Judith S. *Young, Poor, and Pregnant.* New Haven, CT: Yale University Press, 1993, pp. 196-197.

2. Luker, Kristin. *Dubious Conceptions.* Cambridge, MA: Harvard University Press, 1996, pp. 41, 123.

3. Edelman, Hope. *Motherless Daughters.* New York: Dell, Bantam Doubleday, 1974, p. 185.

Chapter 8. We *Can* Affect Their Future

1. De Perla, Jason. "Volunteers: Pro and Con." New York: *New York Times,* April 26, 1997, p. 1

2. Edelman, Hope. *Motherless Daughters.* New York: Dell, Bantam Doubleday, 1974, p. 185.

3. *Teenage Pregnancy.* Arlington, VA: American Association of School Administrators; and New York: Association of Junior Leagues, Inc., 1988, p. 1.

4. Oliver, Jim. St. Petersburg, FL: Interviews. Fall, 1996.

5. Wulf, Steve. "A Generation Excluded." New York: *Time,* October 23, 1995, p. 86.

6. *Elements of Effective Teen Pregnancy Prevention.* Seattle, WA: ASAP, 1996.

7. Homes and Schools visited: Teenagers as Parents Program (TAPP), Bradenton, Florida, Nanette Dizney, Director; Harris Teenage Information Program for Students (TIPS), St. Petersburg, Florida, Pat Hartstein, Director; Maine Children's Home, Waterville, Maine, Sharon Abrams, Director; Our Mother's House, Venice, Florida, Catherine Christiansen, Program Manager; Cyesis, Sarasota, Florida, Barbara White, Social Worker; Solve, Bradenton, Florida, Sister Gloria, Director.

8. Epstein, Michael. Bradenton, FL: Interviews. Spring, 1996.

9. Hawes, Christine. "New Program Offers Alternatives." Sarasota, FL: *Herald-Tribune,* September 23, 1996.

10. Allen-Jones, Patty. "At Risk Teenagers Get a Second Chance."
    Sarasota, FL: *Herald-Tribune,* September 15, 1996, p. A1.

11. Jarmon, Brenda, Ph.D. *A Skill Building Approach for Early
    Adolescents.* Tallahassee, FL: Florida State University, 1992.

12. Reading Pilot: Sarasota Public Schools: Sarasota, Florida, Fall,
    1996, Spring, 1997. Participants: Evelyn Clark, Lois Goodman,
    Evelyn Lerman, Joan Rubinstein, Sarah Sellinger, Roz Surrey,
    Judy Whitman.

13. De Cuevas, J. "Promoting a National Love of Children."
    Cambridge, MA: *Harvard Education Review,* December, 1996,
    pp. 52-58.

14. Witton, Kathleen. Bradenton, FL: Interviews. Spring, 1996.

15. Epstein, op. cit.

16. Tartler, Andy. St. Petersburg, FL: Interviews, April/May, 1996.

17. Buchanan, Constance H. "Welfare Is Not the Problem." Boston,
    MA: *Boston Globe,* July 7, 1996, p. A23.

18. Oliver, op. cit.

19. Hartstein, Pat. St. Petersburg, FL: Interviews. Fall, 1996.

20. Soros, George. "The Capitalist Threat." New York: *Atlantic
    Monthly,* February, 1997, pp. 45-58.

21. Wulf, Steve. "A Generation Excluded." New York: *Time,* October
    23, 1995, p. 86.

22. Dizney, op. cit.

23. Nguyen, P. "Top Cop Hits the Streets." Sarasota, FL: *Sarasota
    Herald-Tribune,* October 31, 1996, p. Al.

24. Hornblower, M. "It Takes a School." New York: *Time,* June 3,
    1996, pp. 36-38.

25. Peirce, Neil R. "Finding Better Ways to Serve People." Sarasota,
    FL: *Herald-Tribune,* September 16, 1996, p. A8.

26. Kamiya, Katherine A. Tallahassee, FL: *Teen Pregnancy Summit
    Report.* FDDC, 1994.

27. Joe, Ronald, Chair. "Impact of Teen Pregnancy in Florida."
    Tallahassee, FL: University of Central Florida, FEECWG, 1995.

28. "Elements of Effective Teen Pregnancy Prevention," op. cit.

29. *A Prospectus for the National Campaign to Prevent Teen
    Pregnancy.* Kean, Hon. Thomas M., Chair. Washington, DC.

Bibliography

Books

Brandon, Nathaniel. *Six Pillars of Self-Esteem*. New York: Bantam, 1994.

_____. *Taking Responsibility*. New York: Simon and Schuster, 1996.

Clinton, Hillary Rodham. *It Takes A Village*. New York: Simon & Schuster, 1996.

Dash, Leon. *When Children Want Children*. New York: William Morrow & Co., 1989.

Durant, Will. *The Story of Philosophy*. New York: Simon and Schuster, 1953.

Edelman, Hope. *Motherless Daughters*. New York: Dell, Bantam Doubleday, 1974.

Lindsay, Jeanne Warren. *Teenage Couples: Expectations and Reality*. Buena Park, CA: Morning Glory Press, 1996.

_____. *Teens Parenting* (Four-book series). Buena Park, CA: Morning Glory Press, 1991.

_____ and Sharon G. Enright. *Books, Babies and School-Age Parents: How to Teach Pregnant and Parenting Teens to Succeed*. Buena Park, CA: Morning Glory Press, 1997.

Luker, Kristin. *Dubious Conceptions.* Cambridge, MA: Harvard
  University Press, 1996.

Males, Mike A. *The Scapegoat Generation.* Monroe, ME: Common
  Courage Press, 1996.

Musick, Judith S. *Young, Poor, & Pregnant.* New Haven, CT: Yale
  University Press, 1993.

Nussbaum, Martha C. *The Fragility of Goodness.* Melbourne, Austra-
  lia: University of Cambridge Press, 1986.

Pipher, Mary. *Reviving Ophelia: Saving the Souls of Adolescent Girls.*
  New York: Ballantine Books, 1995.

Sex and America's Teenagers. New York: The Alan Guttmacher
  Institute, 1994.

Van House, C. L. and Swoszowski, S.M. *Teen Self-Esteem.* Buford,
  GA: Life Lines Press, 1993.

Walsh, Mary R., ed. *The Psychology of Women.* New Haven, CT: Yale
  University Press, 1987.

Weiner, Lynn Y. *From Working Girls to Working Mothers.* Chapel
  Hill, NC: University of North Carolina, 1985.

Reports

Boyer, Debra. "Adolescent Pregnancy: The Role of Sexual Abuse."
  Seattle, WA: *NRCCSA News*, Dec., 1995.

Congressional Quarterly Weekly Report. Washington, DC: Library of
  Congress, Aug. 3, 1996.

Congressional Research Service, Report for Congress. Washington,
  DC: Library of Congress, Aug. 23, 1993.

Elements of Effective Teen Pregnancy Prevention. Seattle, WA:
  Advancing Solutions to Adolescent Pregnancy (ASAP), 1996.

Joe, Ronald, Chair. "Impact of Teen Pregnancy in Florida." Tallahassee, FL: Florida Education and Employment Council for Women
  and Girls (FEECWG), 1995.

Kamiya, Katherine A. *Teen Pregnancy Summit Report.* Tallahassee,
  FL: Florida Developmental Disabilities Council (FDDC), 1994.

Kids Can Cope. Sarasota, FL: Jr. League of Sarasota, Dec. 13, 1995.

Kids Count Data Book. Baltimore, MD: Annie E. Casey Foun., 1996.

_____. 1997.

Maine Kids Count. Augusta, ME: Maine Children's Alliance, 1995-96.

Moore, Kristin, ed. *Facts at a Glance.* Washington, DC: Child Trends, Inc., Jan., 1996.

O'Hare, W. Coor. *Kids Count Data Book.* Baltimore, MD: Annie E. Casey Foundation, 1995.

Teenage Pregnancy. Arlington, VA: American Association of School Administrators; New York: Association of Junior Leagues, 1988.

Vital Statistics Report. Hyattsville, MD: Centers for Disease Control and Prevention, Aug. 23, 1996.

Reviews

Erikson, Kai. "Scandal or Scapegoating?" New York: *New York Times,* review of *Dubious Conceptions* by Kristin Luker, Sept. 1, 1996.

Gleick, Elizabeth. "Surviving Your Teens." New York: *Time,* review of *Reviving Ophelia* by Mary Pipher.

Welentz, Sean. "Jobless and Hopeless." New York: *New York Times,* review of *When Work Disappears* by W. J. Wilson, Sept. 29, 1996.

Articles

"Accidental Pregnancy." St. Petersburg, FL: *Times,* Apr. 28, 1995.

Allen-Jones, Patty. "Program Takes Stock in Children." Sarasota, FL: *Herald-Tribune,* Sept. 17, 1996.

Bennet, James. "Clinton Seeks Help on Proposal over Welfare." Sarasota, FL: *Herald-Tribune,* Jan. 10, 1997.

Brett, Victoria. "Welfare Moms Walk the Wire." Waterville, ME: *Morning Sentinel,* July 5, 1996.

Buchanan, Constance H. "Welfare Is Not the Problem." Boston, MA: *Boston Globe,* July 7, 1996.

Chazin, Suzanne. "Teen Pregnancy: Let's Get Real." Mt. Morris, IL: *Reader's Digest,* Sept., 1996.

Cline, Francis X. "Clinton Signs Bill Cutting Welfare." New York: *New York Times,* Aug. 23, 1996.

"Clinton Announces Teen Welfare Plan." Sarasota, FL: *Herald-Tribune,* May 5, 1996.

De Cuevos, J. "Promoting a National Love of Children." Cambridge, MA: *Harvard Education Review.* Dec., 1996.

Dorrell, Larry D. "A Future at Risk: Children Having Children."

Warrensburg, MO: *Clearing House,* March, 1994.

Douglas, Robert. "Welfare Reform on the Night Shift." Sarasota, FL: *Herald-Tribune,* Sept. 23, 1996.

Ezzard, Martha. "Punishment Won't Curb Teen Pregnancy." Sarasota, FL: *Herald-Tribune,* Sept. 22, 1996.

Geyer, Georgie Anne. "U.S. Students Lost in Ignorance." Universal Press Syndicate, Sarasota, FL: *Herald-Tribune.*

"Giant Companies Cash In on Welfare." New York: *New York Times* News Service, Sept. 16, 1996.

Gibbs, Nancy. "The E. Q. Factor." New York: *Time,* Oct. 2, 1995.

Goldman, D. "Decline of the Nice Guy Quotient." New York: *New York Times Magazine,* Sept. 10, 1995.

Goldsmith, Steve. "Revamping Welfare: Building Lives." New York: *New York Times,* Aug. 4, 1996.

Gonzales, David. "About New York." New York: *New York Times,* Jan. 17, 1996.

Goodman, Ellen. "Marriage Instead of Jail." Boston, MA: *Boston Globe,* Sept. 16, 1996.

Grossfield, Stan. "When Kids Have Kids." Boston, MA: *Boston Globe Magazine,* Oct. 19, 1995.

Hawes, Christine. "New Program Offers Alternatives." Sarasota, FL: *Herald-Tribune*, Sept. 23, 1996.

Herbert, Bob. "Rally for the Defense of Children." Sarasota, FL: *Herald-Tribune,* Apr. 8, 1996.

_____. "Take the A Train." Sarasota, FL: *Herald-Tribune,* Sept. 30, 1996.

Hornblower, Margot. "It Takes a School." New York: *Time,* June 3, 1996.

"Invincible Kids." Washington, DC: *U.S. News and World Report,* Nov. 11, 1996.

Jacobs-Lane, C. and Langenberg, S. "Sunshine State Not Kind to Its Children." Sarasota, FL: *Herald-Tribune,* June 8, 1996.

Jacoby, Jeff. "Welfare Catastrophe?" Boston, MA: *Boston Globe,* Aug. 6, 1996.

Johnson, Derek. "Murders Are a Nice City's Bad News." New York: *New York Times,* June 1, 1996.

Kilborn, Peter T. "Among States Aid to Poor Has Ups and Downs."

Sarasota, FL: *Herald-Tribune,* Feb., 1997.

_____. "States Crafting Ambitious Plans." New York: *New York Times.* Dec. 16, 1996.

Klein, Joe. "The Predator Problem." New York: *Newsweek,* Apr. 29, 1996.

Kuttner, Robert. "A Damaging Welfare Bill." Boston, MA: *Boston Globe,* Aug. 10, 1996.

Males, Mike A. "The Determinants of First Sex by Age 14 in a High-Risk Adolescent Population." Los Angeles, CA: *Protecting Sexually Active Youth Network,* Mar., 1996.

_____. "Poverty, Rape, Adult/Teen Sex: Why Pregnancy Prevention Programs Don't Work." Bloomington, IN: *Phi Delta Kappan,* Spring, 1994.

Mandell, M. "Don't Restrict Sex Education." Sarasota, FL: *Herald-Tribune,* Feb. 24, 1996.

Maxwell, Bill. "Those Who Criticize Can Contribute." Sarasota, FL: *Herald-Tribune,* September 9, 1996.

Mitchell, A. "Clinton Calls for Schooling for Mothers on Welfare." New York: *New York Times,* May 5, 1996.

Musick, Judith. "Poverty and Teen Pregnancy: Implications for Programs." Rutgers, NJ: *Family Life Matters,* Spring, 1995.

Navarro, Mireya. "Teen-Age Mothers Viewed as Abused by Older Men." New York: *New York Times,* May 19, 1996.

"New Study's Findings Contradict Welfare Stereotype." Sarasota, FL: AP, *Herald-Tribune,* Sept. 17, 1996.

"Panel Explores How to Keep Men at Home." Sarasota, FL: *Herald-Tribune,* Sept. 19, 1996.

Peirce, Neil R. "Finding Better Ways to Serve People." Sarasota, FL: *Herald-Tribune,* Sept. 16, 1996.

Phi Delta Kappan. Bloomington, IN: Spring, 1995.

Scales, Peter C. "Nonsensical Beliefs." *Florida Educator,* Winter, 1995/1996.

Pickett, Darla L. "Winslow Teen Parents Beat Odds." Waterville, ME: *Morning Sentinel,* July 22, 1996.

"Pregnant Teens, Adult Fathers Advised to Wed." New York: *New York Times* News Service, Sept. 9, 1996.

Raspberry, William. "Teen Pregnancy's False Dreams." Sarasota, FL:

Herald-Tribune, Sept. 9, 1996.

Ryan, Michael. "Let's Make It Happen." Sarasota, FL: *Herald-Tribune, Parade,* Apr. l7, 1996.

Saltonstall, Polly. "Poor Brace for Welfare Reform." Waterville, ME: *Morning Sentinel,* Aug. 3, 1996.

Samuelson, R. J. "The Elusive Effects of Reform." Boston, MA: *Boston Globe,* Aug. 6, 1996.

Schwartz, Pepper. "New Bonds: Para-Dads, Para-Moms." New York: *New York Times,* Nov. 9, 1995.

Soros, George. "The Capitalist Threat." New York: *Atlantic Monthly,* Feb., 1997, pp. 45-58.

Steinfels, Peter. "Beliefs." New York: *New York Times,* June 1, 1996.

Sweeney, Camille. "Portrait of the American Child." New York: *New York Times Magazine,* Oct. 18, 1996.

"Teenage Sex: Just Say Wait." New York: *U.S. News & World Report,* July 26, 1993.

Uhlenhuth, K. "Emotional Quotient." Sarasota, FL: *Herald-Tribune,* Nov. 8, 1995.

Updike, John. "What Grown-Ups Don't Understand." New York: *New York Times Magazine,* Oct. 8, 1995.

Usdansky, M. L. "Single Motherhood: Stereotypes vs. Statistics." New York: *New York Times,* Feb. 11, 1996.

Wilson, William Jules. "Work." New York: *New York Times Magazine,* Aug. 18, 1996.

Wulf, Steve. "A Generation Excluded." New York: *Time,* Oct. 23, 1995.

Editorials

"A Day to Stand Up for Children." Levine, Jack. Sarasota, FL: *Herald-Tribune,* May 31, 1996.

"Who Stands for Children?" New York: *New York Times,* June 1, 1996.

Index

Abrams, Sharon, 25
AIDS, risk of, 31, 57, 66, 71-73,
    106-107
Anderson, Gael, 38
Boyer, Debra, 44-45, 64
Buchanan, Constance, 116-117,
    156-157
Chappel, Gregg, 151
Character House, 151
Child abuse, 88, 104-105
Child support, 78, 124
Dash, Leon, 54, 55
Dizney, Nanette, 25, 42, 161
Early sex, reasons for, 37-58
Edelman, Hope, 89, 142
Education, 86-87, 136-139, 141-
    142, 147, 148-153
Epstein, Michael, 151, 155
Fathers, absent, 39, 40, 70, 91,
    124, 146

Fathers, older, 33, 45, 58, 68-70,
    126
Fathers, supportive, 75-77, 79
Goldsmith, Steve, 117
Group homes, 153-154
Hartstein, Pat, 118-120, 158
Health, 102-103
Jacoby, Jeff, 117
Jarmon, Brenda, 152
Kamiya, Katherine A., 101
Literacy, 142, 147, 152
Lobbying, 147
Luker, Kristin, 88, 125
Male predators, 45, 58, 68-70,
    126
Male role model, 42, 73, 78, 146
Males, Mike A., 38, 42, 67, 88,
    104
Marriage, 31, 145-146
Maternal neglect, 46-47, 52

Maternal role, 159-160
Media, 158
Medicaid, 22, 24, 34
Menarche, onset of, 56
Mentor, 147, 157-165
Moore, Kristin, 58
Moran, Bea, 54
Mothers, over-protective, 89-91
Musick, Judith S., 38, 41, 62, 81-82, 91
Oliver, Jim, 52, 148, 157-158
Parenting, quality of, 33, 34, 79
Peer pressure, 37, 52-53, 59, 65, 157-158
Pipher, Mary, 77, 101
Poverty, 34, 38, 68, 79, 84-86, 105-106, 126, 146
Pregnancy, intentional, 32, 33, 54-55, 59, 108
Public opinion, 19, 21-23, 29-34, 56-57
Religious belief, 92-93
Resiliency, 50-51, 73
Schilling, Max, 42, 55
School, alternative, 136-139, 141-142, 148-154, 162-163
School, difficulties with, 22
Self-esteem, 24, 25, 37, 66, 77, 161
Serial monogamy, 72

Sex and America's Teenagers, 55, 106
Sex education, 34, 92
Sex, involuntary, 12, 31, 33, 42-45, 58, 61-64, 79, 88, 104
Sex, premarital, 31, 58
Siblings, care of, 47-51
Single parents, 34, 51-52, 59, 71, 78, 145-146, 161
Soros, George, 158-159
Suicide, 101
Tartler, Andy, 155
Teams for Teens, 148
Teen sexual activity, 30-31
Unmarried birthrate, 34, 57-58
Violence, 66-68, 72, 88-89, 103-104
Welfare reform, 115-129
Welfare, 156
Welfare, attitudes toward, 33, 116-127
Welfare, limits of, 22, 24
Witton, Kathleen, 25, 153
Work, 22, 24, 116-129, 156-157, 160
Working poor, 126
Worries, 99-113
Wulf, Steve, 148
Younger teens, advice for, 109-113

About the Author

Evelyn Lerman has it all — writing experience, interest in children and the expertise to work with them, and the knowledge about incorporating the research data into her personal findings from her interviews with many teenage mothers.

Lerman has been a non-fiction writer most of her life. From an early interest in interviewing and writing for newspapers and yearbooks in high school, she majored in journalism in college. While there, she worked on the newspapers and yearbooks, and after graduation, became the writer, editor, and everything-in-chief of the family business trade journal for ten years. During her teaching career, she authored innumerable curriculum units and contributed to a book on writing.

Lerman's graduate degrees include one in education, another in human development.

Lerman, who retired from her work with the schools, still teaches writing. *Teen Moms: The Pain and the Promise* reveals her deep love for young people and her expertise in helping her readers empathize with the world of very young mothers, a world of poverty, abuse — and hope.

ICES FROM MORNING GLORY PRESS

*...ND SCHOOL-AGE PARENTS: How to Teach
...enting Teens to Succeed* by Jeanne Warren Lindsay
...ns Enright, Ph.D. How-to guide for anyone who
...age parents.

...I TEEN PREGNANCY: Choices, Dreams, Decisions.
...nant teens—help with decisions, moving on toward goals.

*...NT? ADOPTION IS AN OPTION: Making an Adoption
...I a Child.* Encourages pregnant teens to consider an adoption
...s well as a parenting plan.

...NS PARENTING—Your Pregnancy and Newborn Journey.
...ow to take care of yourself and your newborn. For pregnant teens.
Available in "regular" (RL 6), Easier Reading (RL 3), and Spanish.

TEENS PARENTING—Your Baby's First Year.
TEENS PARENTING—The Challenge of Toddlers.
TEENS PARENTING—Discipline from Birth to Three.
Three how-to-parent books especially for teenage parents.

TEEN DADS: Rights, Responsibilities and Joys. Parenting book for teenage fathers.

DO I HAVE A DADDY? A Story About a Single-Parent Child.
Picture/story book especially for children with only one parent. Also available in Spanish, *¿Yo tengo papá?*

SCHOOL-AGE PARENTS: The Challenge of Three-Generation Living. Help for families when teen daughter (or son) has a child.

WILL THE DOLLARS STRETCH? Four short stories about teen parents moving out on their own. Includes check register exercises.

TEENAGE COUPLES—Expectations and Reality. For professionals, research involving survey of 3700 teenagers.

BREAKING FREE FROM PARTNER ABUSE. Guidance for victims of domestic violence.

Novels by Marilyn Reynolds: *DETOUR FOR EMMY* (teen pregnancy); *TOO SOON FOR JEFF* (reluctant teen father); *BUT WHAT ABOUT ME?* (acquaintance rape); *TELLING* (molestation); *BEYOND DREAMS* (six short stories about teen crises), and *BABY HELP* (novel focusing on teen partner abuse).

Visit your bookstore — or order directly from Morning Glory Press
6595 San Haroldo Way, Buena Park, CA 90620. 714/828-1998.
Free catalog on request.

About the Author

Evelyn Lerman has it all — writing experience, interest in children and the expertise to work with them, and the knowledge about incorporating the research data into her personal findings from her interviews with many teenage mothers.

Lerman has been a non-fiction writer most of her life. From an early interest in interviewing and writing for newspapers and yearbooks in high school, she majored in journalism in college. While there, she worked on the newspapers and yearbooks, and after graduation, became the writer, editor, and everything-in-chief of the family business trade journal for ten years. During her teaching career, she authored innumerable curriculum units and contributed to a book on writing.

Lerman's graduate degrees include one in education, another in human development.

Lerman, who retired from her work with the schools, still teaches writing. *Teen Moms: The Pain and the Promise* reveals her deep love for young people and her expertise in helping her readers empathize with the world of very young mothers, a world of poverty, abuse — and hope.

OTHER RESOURCES FROM MORNING GLORY PRESS

BOOKS, BABIES AND SCHOOL-AGE PARENTS: How to Teach Pregnant and Parenting Teens to Succeed by Jeanne Warren Lindsay and Sharon Githens Enright, Ph.D. How-to guide for anyone who works with teenage parents.

SURVIVING TEEN PREGNANCY: Choices, Dreams, Decisions. For all pregnant teens—help with decisions, moving on toward goals.

PREGNANT? ADOPTION IS AN OPTION: Making an Adoption Plan for a Child. Encourages pregnant teens to consider an adoption plan as well as a parenting plan.

TEENS PARENTING—Your Pregnancy and Newborn Journey. How to take care of yourself and your newborn. For pregnant teens. Available in "regular" (RL 6), Easier Reading (RL 3), and Spanish.

TEENS PARENTING—Your Baby's First Year.
TEENS PARENTING—The Challenge of Toddlers.
TEENS PARENTING—Discipline from Birth to Three.
Three how-to-parent books especially for teenage parents.

TEEN DADS: Rights, Responsibilities and Joys. Parenting book for teenage fathers.

DO I HAVE A DADDY? A Story About a Single-Parent Child. Picture/story book especially for children with only one parent. Also available in Spanish, *¿Yo tengo papá?*

SCHOOL-AGE PARENTS: The Challenge of Three-Generation Living. Help for families when teen daughter (or son) has a child.

WILL THE DOLLARS STRETCH? Four short stories about teen parents moving out on their own. Includes check register exercises.

TEENAGE COUPLES—Expectations and Reality. For professionals, research involving survey of 3700 teenagers.

BREAKING FREE FROM PARTNER ABUSE. Guidance for victims of domestic violence.

Novels by Marilyn Reynolds: *DETOUR FOR EMMY* (teen pregnancy); *TOO SOON FOR JEFF* (reluctant teen father); *BUT WHAT ABOUT ME?* (acquaintance rape); *TELLING* (molestation); *BEYOND DREAMS* (six short stories about teen crises), and *BABY HELP* (novel focusing on teen partner abuse).

Visit your bookstore — or order directly from Morning Glory Press
6595 San Haroldo Way, Buena Park, CA 90620. 714/828-1998.
Free catalog on request.